SPIKE ISLAND

To Chuck & Anne

Michael Martin

SPIKE ISLAND

saints, felons and famine

MICHAEL MARTIN

NONSUCH

Dedicated to
Eamon and Elizabeth Martin (RIP)
my beloved parents,
who planted the seeds of inspiration.

First published 2007

Nonsuch Publishing
73 Lower Leeson Street
Dublin 2, Ireland
www.nonsuch-publishing.com

Nonsuch Publishing is an imprint of NPI Media Group

© Michael Martin, 2007

The right of Michael Martin to be identified as the Author of this work has been
asserted in accordance with the Copyrights, Designs and Patents Act 1988.

British Library Cataloguing in Publication Data.
A catalogue record for this book is available from the British Library.

ISBN 978 1 84588 910 4

Typesetting and origination by NPI Media Group
Printed and bound in Great Britain by Athenaeum Press Ltd., Gateshead, Tyne & Wear

Contents

Acknowledgements

The writing of any book and the compilation of historical information requires a great deal of time, effort and work. While the author may be immediately attributed with the credit for his or her creation, there are always those in the background without whom the project would never have seen the light of day. In my case, I want to acknowledge the continual support, encouragement and tolerance of my wife, Geraldine. I am eternally grateful for your help, thank you. My two sons Ken and Gary also offered encouragement of a different type, from a different perspective. Thank you both.

During my research in Australia I was assisted in the most practical fashion with advice and sometimes accommodation by the people of Bothwell, Tasmania and the guides, historians, and officials of Port Arthur, in particular, Richard Lord and Susan Hood. My thanks also to my extended families, cousins of the Nealon family and close friends Josh and Maureen Sheils, as their family provided me with much needed R&R in Brisbane.

My sincere thanks also to Tom O'Neill of the Irish Prison Service; Tom Foster, deputy governor of Spike Island; Cobh Town Council; Cobh Museum; local historian John Hennessy; Professor Dermot Keogh, Dr Damien Bracken and Gabriel Doherty of the History Department of University College Cork; Dr Carmel Quinlan, Dr Andrew McCarthy and Dr Michael Cosgave of the same institution; Tom McSweeney and Marcus Connaughton of RTÉ Cork, who valued my research and brought it to life on national radio; Maureen Mahon, who understood the demands of the scribe and assisted me greatly in my working life so that I could concentrate on the research and the writing. Finally, thank you to my many friends, family and neighbours of Cobh and elsewhere who are far too numerous to mention.

I

Cork Harbour:
Home to Spike Island

Spike Island. Fourteen centuries and more. Silent, knowing and bearing witness. A fortress island, a sanctuary, a place of learning, an island paradise, a living hell. It has been all these things. It remains aloof in the midst of comings and goings, developments and change. Unimpressed and unchanged itself, Spike Island is a repository of Irish heritage, a place reflecting many aspects of Ireland's history. The best of it and the worst of it. The gifted, the Holy. The cruel, the inhuman. The famine.

There are numerous other islands of various sizes and shapes in Cork Harbour. Among them are the Rocky, Haulbowline, Corkbeg, Hop, Fota, Little and Great Islands and there is even a Rat and a Hare Island. Today, these islands and the encircling mainland reflect modern usage of the harbour as an industrial base and a leisure activity area. Many of the big names in the

pharmaceutical industry operate research development and manufacturing plants on the western side of
the harbour near Ringaskiddy and Shanbally. On the
eastern side at Whitegate and Aghada, an oil refinery
and an electricity generating plant help feed Ireland's
twenty-first-century energy requirements.

The island of Haulbowline, in the middle of the
harbour, is home to the Irish Navy. Despite their small
fleet they operate a number of ultra modern vessels and
are full partners in the operation and running of the
National Maritime College nearby. This college uses
leading 'state of the art' technology to educate students
about life at sea. Simulation of storms, fires and evacu-
ation by lifeboat in any number of situations are all
features of the training that takes place there.

At East Ferry on the eastern end of Great Island, a
different type of training is provided. Sailors young and
old learn sailing skills at one of the foremost training
centres, in the very same harbour that founded the
concept of organised sailing for leisure. In 1720 the
'Water Club' was founded on Haulbowline Island. It
was to eventually become the Royal Cork Yacht Club
and remains the first and therefore the oldest yacht
club in the world. Although now situated at Cross-
haven, the club was based in Cobh for many years
before moving to its present location in the mid-
1960s. Today at East Ferry the sailors of tomorrow
are taught how to tack, track and navigate in yachts,

cruisers and punts, always applying the principles of enjoyment and safety.

The town of Cobh attracts thousands of visitors each year. People come from scores of different countries to learn of the harbour's past, its heritage, and its islands. Each of these islands has its own distinctive story to tell, making a fascinating collection. Where else on earth would you find a cluster of so many, in such close proximity, that were overlooked by pre-Christian cairns, that hosted seventh-century monasteries, twelfth-century military posts, fourteenth-century governors, eighteenth-century penal settlements, military armoury magazines, castles, keeps, Martello towers and the magnificent nineteenth-century Neo-Gothic architecture of St Colman's Cathedral. The islands in this harbour have witnessed the ravages of invasion, absorbed the tears of tragic famine and been tread upon by young, grey-faced soldiers destined for wars in foreign places. They have heard the wails of those dispatched in chains to distant prisons and felt the ray of hope in emigrant expectations.

Cobh is situated on the largest and most important of these islands. Its winding streets cling to ancient cliffs and hills. The entire town overlooks the grace and majesty of what is said to be second largest and most beautiful harbour in the world. This claim to being the second largest is not unique. In Great Britain they say it's the harbour of Poole. In Canada, they say Halifax.

Nobody seems to dispute that Sydney, Australia is the largest but have all the harbours of Asia, Alaska and other parts of the world been compared? Doubts remain.

Pivotal to the history of the town of Cobh (or Queenstown as it was known from 1849 to 1921) was its role as an important military port, where hundreds of thousands of soldiers, sailors and Defence Department officials of the British establishment were stationed. There was a British military presence in the harbour for approximately eight centuries. The town was an embarkation point for troops onward bound for conflicts such as the Crimean and Boer Wars. Earlier, large fleets had gathered there, awaiting the Royal Navy to provide sea-escorting duties during the trying years of the Napoleonic Wars. During the First World War, an American fleet of ships also came, and over the years, hundreds of shipping company clerks and executives operated the shipping line companies that flourished when Cobh was a hub of transatlantic travel.

Millions of emigrants, often fleeing political or economic oppression and even starvation, fled through Cobh. Presidents of Ireland, and of the United States, Queen Victoria and Laurel and Hardy have passed through these streets.

Cruise liners still visit, making their way through the narrow entrance of the harbour. Navigating around Spike Island to squeeze between Haulbowline and Great

Island, they berth at a deepwater quay that was honed out of bedrock and developed in 1882. The passengers are disgorged and often, in the rush of modern tourism, they are left blissfully unaware of the heritage and history of Cobh and Cork Harbour, and of its timeless links with events that shaped peoples and nations throughout the world.

Cobh and Cork Harbour is an area of maritime fascination. Take, for example, the stories of Phoenician invasion; thirty-two boats filled with thirty men each, under the command of a colourful Phoenician prince, landed here 1,200 years before Christianity was to emerge from the same region as they did.

There are stories of invasions by the Celts, fearsome warriors who overran the mighty city of Rome in the fifth century. Their ancient gravesite (or cairn) on Currabinny Hill, in the south-west corner of the harbour, is a reminder of their pre-Christian period presence. One must be captivated too by the idea of Christian monks on Spike Island as early as the seventh century, going about their simple daily tasks in devotion and humility.

The harbour also saw the arrival of Vikings, who engaged in rape, pillage and plunder, up and into Cork. Leaving, and then returning to merge with the local population, the influence and sea experience of the Vikings eventually encouraged the opening up of new sea lanes and routes, facilitating better trade, new markets and maritime commerce.

The army of King Henry II was sent with the endorsement of the world's only ever English Pope, Adrian IV. They recognised immediately the value of the harbour and so they didn't leave for eight centuries.

The Spanish Armada sailed the south coast, outside the reach of the cannon batteries, placed, in the 1540s, on the western side of the only entrance to Cork Harbour. They were later augmented by batteries on the eastern side and, later still, further batteries at Haulbowline and Great Island. Had they got past those cannons it might have changed the course of Irish history.

Cobh and the magnificent harbour it graces has played host, in the days of sail, to those ships that searched out and probed new lands, that crossed angry oceans and rounded fearsome capes. It has been occupied by the military and naval might of a past world power. It has witnessed the tragic drain of entire generations of emigrants, millions of whom set out with hope and determination often expecting never to see their homeland again. They waved goodbye from creaking decks as they slipped away to find a better life and a prosperous future. Every single one who left this place passed by the silent brooding presence of Spike Island, before exiting into the often unforgiving Atlantic Ocean.

It is this island in the middle of Cork Harbour that embodies the most extraordinarily diverse background of all islands in the area. Prisoners, soldiers, sailors, governors, schoolteachers, monks, abbots, convicts and patriots have all occupied Spike over a vast tract of time beginning as early as the seventh century AD, when a monastery was founded there. To each group the island meant something different. It could be a place of quiet spiritual contemplation or a location of isolation, cruelty and death. The island has numerous abiding themes; ecclesiastical, penal, military, social, famine and political heritage. Of them all, the early period of the monastery, the connections with the famed John Mitchel and, most especially, the inextricable links between this island and some of the consequences of the famine, demand our attention.

2

The Island

Long recognised by the British as a location of military strategic importance, Spike Island, at various times through its history, was also used as a place of detention. Records show that many individuals, young and old, who were sent there as convicts in the mid-nineteenth century to serve a supposedly finite sentence, never left it.[1] This contrasts sharply with the earlier historical period of the island when its monastery may have produced manuscripts of important ecclesiastical value.

This book examines some of Spike Island's tumultuous background. It will show that, by virtue of its location and diversity of use over many years, Spike Island should be considered a place of significant historical importance. In pursuit of this, I will explore any possible links between the influence of the founder of the monasteries on Spike Island and Lismore, and the later spiritual reform movement in Ireland. In stark contrast to the ecclesiastical period on the island was the use of the prison as a centre of detention for convicts, particularly during the famine. Although officially listed as dangerous criminals, felons and convicts, the reality is that many of those who found themselves incarcerated on Spike Island from 1847 were there as a direct result of the famine and its effect on the island of Ireland. Some had stolen food to feed their families; others, sheep or pigs to do the same. One man on Spike Island was there awaiting transportation for stealing potatoes. Yet others were there because they were guilty of the crime of vagrancy. Their situations and how they came about will be examined and compared to the earlier, contrasting history of the Island.

Spike Island is situated in one of the finest natural harbours in the world. Cork Harbour is magnificent. The gentle rolling hills of the mainland encircle and protect the scattering of islands. Enclosed in the natural formation of the harbour, these islands are in the estuary of the river Lee, which rises in the beautiful area of Gougane Barra in West Cork. Some are hardly islands any more; land reclamation and natural silting have left places like Fota and Little Island directly accessible from the mainland. Golf courses, industrial complexes, food outlets, housing developments and luxurious hotels create a diversity of modern architecture and atmosphere.

While it is as yet unspoiled by such modern developments, it is Spike Island that offers the most diverse range of imagery. Enveloped in isolation in the middle of the lower harbour, contrasting themes abound there. It has been considered by some to have been a holy island for over a thousand years; monks working, praying and reflecting out there in a world removed from the present by over fourteen centuries. Perhaps it was a place of fear in the ninth century when the arrival of the Vikings into Cork Harbour struck terror into those who may have been their targets. On other occasions it was a place of comfort; to those who were responsible for the defence of the realm when Ireland was a part of the empire, it was a place of power and protection. A formidable fortress with guns trained both outside and inside the harbour. Spike was also a place of separation and detachment, keeping those caught up in circumstances beyond their control confined and alone, facing years of being apart from their families, often on the other side of the world. This is a place of good and bad themes and of right and wrong.

The island itself almost straddles the entrance to Cork Harbour. Ships, immediately on entering the port from the open sea, are confronted head on with Spike. The natural deep water channel that leads from the river Lee to the mouth of the harbour circumvents the island so that any vessels sailing to or from Cork or Cobh cannot but navigate around it. Since there is only one gateway to and from the harbour itself, it is unavoidable not to see Spike Island whether entering or leaving. Millions of people have done so over the years. The island can look beautiful, particularly in the sunshine, with its green slopes and the scattering of small intimate beaches around its shoreline. On other days it looks dark and brooding, with the ever-present long, low walls that mark the outer ramparts of the fortress that crowns the landscaped island.

The earliest indication of activity on Spike Island comes from the *Lives of the Saints*, a series of manuscripts that outline the life and times of a variety of ecclesiastical figures. The *Lives of Saint Declan and Mochuda*[2] outlines the background to the building of a monastery on Spike Island in AD 635. It was established by St Carthage (Mochuda) also referred to as St Carthach. There are no overground physical remains of the monastery today, although under the Planning Acts the western side of the island has been identified as having a 'potential' archaeological site.

St Carthage was born in Kerry and had established an important monastery at Rahan in County Offaly. This appears to have been a large monastic settlement with over eighty monks. Having spent many years there, St Carthage and his followers were run out of Rahan by a native group of clerics in the area. The reason for this expulsion is not entirely clear and it seems strange that a well-established monastic group should be driven out en masse in this way.

It is possible that St Carthage was ejected from Rahan because of a doctrinal dispute but there is no specific reason mentioned in the *Lives*. Inter-monastic warfare was not uncommon in Ireland during the so-called period of 'Saints and Scholars'. It must be remembered that monastic appointments of abbots and leaders were often chosen from among the most powerful families of a region. There was a fusion of power and religion and so alliances between powerful, wealthy families and particular monasteries were commonplace. Not surprisingly, disputes among monasteries were very often linked to political dynastic families and their rivalries; pitched battles over property, resources and land were common enough at this time. Monasteries rose up against each other in full military battles. Monks were killed, maimed and injured by other monks, supposedly in the name of religion but more often in pursuit of power and territory. Even 200 years later at the height of the Viking raids there were some periods during which the number of Irish monks killed by the Vikings was only exceeded by the number killed by other Irish monks.[3] It will probably never really be known why Carthage fled from Offaly to Munster. However, the *Lives* recount that he did flee, and having set up the monastery on Spike Island, he eventually set up another one at Lismore. This monastery became famous well beyond the boundaries of County Waterford, where it is located.

The later importance of Lismore suggests a high regard in ecclesiastical circles for the work of St Carthage. He was noted for his piety and insistence on simplicity. His style of devotion and doctrinal ethics seems to have been revered at Lismore by his followers for many centuries after he died. In 1903, over 1,200 years after his death, he was made principal patron of Lismore.[4] Over this period, Lismore had become a noted centre of study and ecclesiastical importance.

In the years after his death, clerics of Lismore were to become leading influences in one of the most significant reform movements of the late eighth and the ninth centuries. This movement was known as the Céli Dé and it was primarily associated with a monastery at Tallaght in Co. Dublin. It was a spiritual reform movement that espoused the virtue of simplicity and a rejection of the laicisation of monasteries that had become a feature of European monastic life.[5] One of those noted for the founding of this movement in Ireland is MacOige of Lismore (d. 753).[6]

In his book on spiritual reform, Peter O'Dwyer states that the movement began in the south of Ireland in a district that included Lismore, and that the Tallaght documents look back with great respect at men like MacOige of Lismore and Mocholmoc Ua Liathain, also of Lismore.[7] He also considers the suggestions of Professor Kathleen Hughes and Miss Sanderlin regarding the significance of Lismore monks in compiling early and contemporary sources to write *The Litany of the Pilgrim Saints*, and he poses the question: 'Did the devotion to Irish saints so noted in Tallaght begin in Lismore and find its way to Tallaght to return once again to Lismore?'[8]

Was the influence of the man who founded the monastery on Spike the basis of the devotion espoused by monastic successors at Lismore? Were their approaches to prayer and reform indicative of the type of worship that Carthage established when he set up Lismore? It seems reasonable to suggest that his ethos could have had some influence on the distinctive culture that the Waterford monastery was later noted for. He had, after all, founded this monastery and was himself known for his spiritual approach to prayer, work and poverty. T.M. Charles-Edwards, an eminent professor of History at the University of Cambridge refers to the 'Rule of St Carthach', which includes instructions for Céli Dé, meaning 'clients of God'.[9] This was the name taken by the Tallaght reform movement that emerged in the second quarter of the seventh century about ninety to one hundred years after the death of Carthage.

Questions must be asked as to how and why the founder of one of the most important ecclesiastical centres in Ireland came to found a monastery on Spike Island. This connection would certainly confer an importance upon the monastic settlement of Spike

Island not previously considered. How Carthage came to get the island is described in the *Life of St Mochuda of Lismore*:

Another time again a King of Munster, Cathal Mac Aodha, in the region of Cuirche, was a sufferer from a combination of complaints – he was deaf, lame and blind, and when Mochuda came to see him the King and his friends prayed the Saint to cure him.

Mochuda therefore prayed for him and made the sign of the cross on his eyes and ears and immediately he was healed of all his maladies – he heard and saw perfectly, and Cathal gave extensive lands to God and Mochuda forever, scil: – Oilean cathail and Ros-Beg and Ros-Mor and Inis-Pic. Mochuda placed a religious community on Ros-Beg to build there a church in honour of God. Mochuda himself commenced to build a church on Inis-Pic and he remained there a whole year. [On his departure] Mochuda left there – in the monastery of Inis-Pic – to watch over it, in his stead, and to keep it in perfect order – the three disciples whom we have already named (scil: – the three sons of Nascon, i.e. Goban, a bishop, Srafan, a priest, and holy Laisren) together with the saintly bishop Dardomaighen, (who had conferred orders on them in presence of Mochuda) and forty monks. Thereupon Mochuda returned to Rahan. That island we have mentioned, scil:– Inis-Pic, is a most holy place in which an exceedingly devout community constantly dwell.[10]

The references in this manuscript are extremely interesting. An 'exceedingly devout community' is described, seemingly moulded by the presence and influence of Carthage, who stayed there for a whole year. The description of those leaders he left behind as 'disciples' suggests his role as a teacher and authority on whatever religious practices they pursued. Were these the same instructive practices that marked out Carthage as a particularly devout Christian, by those who wrote about his stewardship of Lismore? Given the significant influence of Lismore, which he founded, it is reasonable to suggest that any monastery founded by this man must be of some historical and ecclesiastical importance, but were the devotional ethics that later marked Lismore as a centre of ecclesiastical excellence first practiced at Spike Island? Many questions arise as to his motives and methods but, given the passage of time and the scant nature of evidence, they are very difficult to answer. However, if Carthage was a religious leader of importance at the time, it is probable that he encouraged not just devotional practice but religious writings.

Spike Island, in the middle of Cork Harbour, is still a place of solitude where contemplation and reflection comes easy; it is not difficult to envision what it must have been like fourteen centuries ago. One can imagine it as a place where monks, seeking a greater understanding of the ways of God and his works, might have been prompted to inscribe their thoughts. The older texts certainly suggest it was a place that would be 'most holy'.

3

The Liber Creaturarum

In 1953 a famous ecclesiastical manuscript called the *Liber de ordine creaturarum*, which was for centuries thought to be of Spanish origin and written by St Isidore of Seville, was noted by Spanish expert Manuel C. Díaz y Díaz to almost certainly have been written in Ireland. This work describes God and his Great Plan for the universe. Marina Smyth quotes Charles W. Jones who describes it as:

A work of magnificent conception. Intertwining spatial and temporal dimensions, it is a bold attempt at describing God's grand plan for the universe he created, from the supercelestial heavens above the firmament to hell below the earth, from the timeless existence of God before creation till life everlasting beyond the end of time. This is through and through a religious work, giving a careful account of all that exists from a Christian perspective – for its author the only true perspective. It is a fascinating and many faceted treatise revealing much about the milieu in which it was written.[11]

Smyth points out that Díaz y Díaz bases his argument on the reliance of the document on a text written in Ireland in AD 655, *De mirabilibus sacrae scripturae*, but he accepts the possibility that it could also have been written in England. On the other hand she points out that Paul Grosjean already suggested in 1955 that the author of the *Liber de ordine creaturarum* was 'associated with the foundations of St Carthach, that is, mainly Lismore (founded in 636), Rahan and Clonfertmulloe…'[12]

Many of the scholars quoted by Marina Smyth agree that this most important of manuscripts was written in Ireland, and also that it relied heavily on the *De mirabilibus*, which has been suggested by some, because of its tidal information, to have been written near the Shannon. However, Marina Smyth has proposed 'another possible place for composition: the more southern coastal area of Cork Harbour, where a monastery said to have been founded by St Carthach was located on Spike Island'.[13] These scholars at least raise the possibility of the monastery on Spike Island being of enormous historical and ecclesiastical significance.

Locally, in East Cork, there is the continuing impression of Spike Island having been a place of religious importance. At time of writing there have been no archaeological surveys done on Spike Island, but a survey may give clues as to whether monk scribes laboured on this island; perhaps there are remnants of tools used for writing, such as dyes or inkwells. There is no sign of a monastery above ground, but if a survey was to take place who knows what might be found.

Apart from the literary sources of the monastery there is anecdotal and other evidence. In December 2006, a seventy-nine-year-old lady, Mrs Phil Lynch from Cloyne in County Cork, recounted a story told to her by her grandmother. The grandmother said that as a little girl she used to be taken on some Sundays to Spike Island from East Ferry. She was always told they were visiting the 'Holy Island'. Clearly Spike Island was perceived to be something special.

One of a pair of late eighteenth-century paintings of Spike Island[14] depicts buildings and towers that evidently did not survive the later upgrading of the fortifications and the construction of the star-shaped fort, which commenced in the 1790s. The second island is named 'Ballymacuttah', which suggests a connection with Mochuda and the painting does indeed show what looks like ecclesiastical ruins. Peter Murray writes that 'Ballymacuttah' is not listed as a name in any of the records of Cork Harbour and further suggests this may be Cork Beg Island.[15] Neither of the islands shown is totally accurate but one can at least infer that both of the islands depicted closely resemble the islands purported to have been given to Carthage where he set up a community of monks on one and on the other, Spike, a monastery.

Another problem in locating these ecclesiastical ruins on Spike is that they are in a position where there was a former fort called Westmoreland, the forerunner of the structure commenced round 1792 and given the same name on completion. This earlier structure is identified and visible on a map showing the building in progress of the latter Fort Westmoreland in 1809.[16] To date it is only this secondary literary and anecdotal evidence that provides information on the monastic period of Spike Island. There remains however the exciting possibility of Spike Island having been the source of this famous document and a centre of spiritual contemplation.

Whatever the scarcity of primary source material for the monastic period, there is even less for the period 200 years later, covering the Viking Raids of Cork between AD 822 and 835. It has been suggested that this lack of evidence was a consequence of the island being attacked by Vikings.

The Viking raids started in Ireland in the late eighth and early ninth centuries, the first taking place at Rathlin Island off the north coast in AD 795. In the ensuing years, raids took place along the north-west,

west, south-west and south coasts, reaching Cork Harbour in AD 822.[17] A second raid of Cork in AD 835 suggests that the Vikings had profited from the first one and it was therefore worthwhile for them to return. On the second occasion the Viking raiders settled in Cork and established their own town within sight of the monastic city of St Finbar.

During this period many island communities were attacked along Irish coastal waters, among them, Rathlin Island, Tory Island, and most famously the Skellig Islands off County Kerry. We know that many monks of the Skellig monastic community were put to death on this occasion, but no evidence has yet come to light that the Vikings attacked Spike. But does this mean that they never did? Given its prominence at the entrance of the harbour, and that any vessel coming into or out of Cork Harbour must navigate around it, one would have expected that Spike Island would be a primary target. Whether it was or was not remains a matter of intriguing speculation. James Coleman, HMC, MRSA, writing in 1893 explains the lack of evidence thus:

From the seventh century, when St Carthage flourished and Spike Island became through him the holy isle which the above quoted document shows[18] it to have been, a complete blank occurs in its historical records, right down to the twelfth century. This blank is to be attributed, no doubt, to the disappearance of its monastery, which latter in all probability was destroyed by the Danes.[19]

Coleman contends that the likelihood of the monastery being of a wooden structure would further mitigate against any records or evidence surviving.

Given its geographical location and its command of the only entrance in and out of the harbour, the probability of an attack on Spike Island by the Vikings is quite high but until some new evidence emerges it will never really be known exactly what happened when the Vikings raided the area. Hopefully a structured archaeological dig will reveal something in the future. It does seem highly unlikely that during the initial raids on Cork Harbour, the Vikings would have ignored the possible plunder of a monastery. One of the primary functions of these raids was to gather any booty they could find and monasteries had traditionally provided rich pickings for them.

After the ninth century there is ample evidence that the Island was occupied. The Normans arrived in Waterford in the late 1160s. An invitation by an Irish chieftain and the granting of overlordship by a Christian pope were the two main factors in the arrival and subsequent colonisation of Ireland by the Normans.

A fierce personal rivalry between two Irish chieftains, O'Rourke and McMorrow, had seen the latter go abroad in search of some external aid to help defeat his rival. A meeting sought with Henry II of England did not materialise, but the Earl of Pembroke, later known as Strongbow agreed to travel to Ireland in return for certain privileges and payment including the hand of McMorrow's daughter in marriage. Strongbow helped McMorrow in his struggle and in turn won the hand of Aoife. He began to consolidate his power in Ireland and it was not long before Henry II, cautious of this rise in status, came to Ireland himself to assert his authority and copper-fasten the loyalty of Strongbow. Much earlier, in 1155, on Henry's accession to the throne, the Pope of the day, Adrian IV, granted overlordship of Ireland to Henry, thus giving papal approval to the seizing of Ireland.

Over ensuing years the acquisition of lands by Henry's vassals was a persistent issue. County Cork and Spike Island became Anglo-Norman property under a charter of Henry II, during which time there still appears to have been a church on the Island. James Coleman quotes from the *Journal of the Royal Society of Antiquaries of Ireland part I, 1892*:

That amongst the Cork grants made to St Thomas's Abbey, in 1178, were the church of St Ruisen on Inis Pic [Spike Island] and, in 1270, St Nicholas's chapel in the city of Cork, on condition that the abbey should pay yearly to St Fin Barre's church five Nummi Anglici and one pound of wax. St Ruisen of Spike Island memory, this paper adds, was the same person as Ross, son of Tricem who is alleged to have taken part in the compilation of the Senchus More in St Patrick's Time – according to the Martyrology of Donegal, under the date of April 7th. [20]

Given that Pope Adrian IV had granted overlordship of Ireland to Henry II sixteen years before he arrived in 1171, it is not surprising that churches were spared in the initial colonisation of Ireland. An occupying army would hardly plunder the places of worship associated with their benefactors. Whatever British military presence was on Spike Island in the twelfth century, it would not have duly interfered with the church or monastery that was already there at the time.

Awareness of Spike in Rome is testified by the fact that the island was reaffirmed in 1199 by Pope Innocent III, 564 years after the monastery was founded. This was during a period of considerable co-operation between the church in Ireland and the Normans. Perhaps some issue or question arose over the ownership of the island. Coleman writes:

In the ensuing years from the twelfth to the late eighteenth century the lands on the island changed hands on many occasions There was ownership ascribed to Thomas Pyke and in 1490 Maurice Ronan.

Later the Roches and Galweys of Cork who lost possession of it in the so called 'rebellion' of 1641 and failed to recover it again from Charles II, The Earl of Albemarie who conveyed 56 acres of it to William Smith of Ballymore in 1698. In 1700 the protestant Bishop of Cork and Ross wrote Spike was of the parish of Great Island and in 1774 ecclesiastically a particle of the barony of Imokilly.[21]

If the monastery had been in continuous operation for over five centuries, then even at this point, there had to have been considerable evidence of its presence, besides any existing buildings. Where are the monks who died there buried? There must have been a monastic cemetery somewhere on the island. Again, archaeological research is desperately needed on Spike Island if the full heritage and importance of the place is to be realised. It would seem that, despite the ownership and ecclesiastical connections of the island between the twelfth and the seventeenth centuries, it remained at times unoccupied. Local belief subscribes to the idea that it had become a place of smugglers during such periods.

During the time of the American Revolution a fortified battery was planned, and construction began in 1779. It appears this work was abandoned in 1783 but nine years later work on a new, star-shaped fortress began under the design of General Charles Vallency.[22]

4

Changing Usage

Before this upgrading of Spike Island's fortifications, it may have served a dramatically different purpose to its monastic origins. The island is believed to have been used as a holding centre for the 'transplantation' of thousands of Irish people to the West Indies.[23]

As a consequence of the Cromwellian campaign in Ireland in 1649, a policy of transplantation emerged whereby Irish Catholics were given the option of being put to the sword or be sent to the West Indies. This policy came about as a result of the fears of Cromwell and others that the large Catholic population of Ireland was a potential threat to the Parliamentarians who had just won the English Civil War. Cromwell saw the predominant Catholic population as a potential army that would provide support to the Royalist side in the Civil War, with the underlying threat of an invasion of England. The activities of Cromwell during his brief visit to Ireland in 1649 would probably be referred to today as 'ethnic cleansing'. Catholic priests were hunted down and hanged; nuns and religious orders raped and killed; churches burned with congregations inside. These are the activities that Ireland associates with Cromwell. One of his worst atrocities was the slaughter of hundreds, if not thousands, of people in Drogheda, where no quarter was given to anyone, even if they surrendered. The city had dared to refuse him and his troops access to their walled city, where Cromwell believed a number of rebels responsible for an attack on his army were hiding out. In response, he laid siege to the city for two days, after which he breached the walls and entered the city enraged. Accounts vary as to the number who died; some record over 3,000 citizens were put to the sword. Whatever the number, the city streets were reputedly like rivers of blood. Modern readers will be surprised to discover that this notorious event occurred on 11 September, a date now synonymous with terrorism and tragedy, following the deaths of more than 3,000 people in the attacks on New York's World Trade Centre in 2001.

In addition to the killing and displacing of the Catholics of Ireland, another method adopted by Cromwell was 'transplantation'. This involved removing thousands of Irish people from their homes and lands, and sending them out of the country. Sean O'Callaghan writes that claims regarding the number of people transplanted and sold into slavery during this period vary, ranging from 12,000 to 40,000 men, women and children. Most of these individuals were shipped to Barbados for deployment as indentured servants or slaves.[24]

This method of 'transplantation' was targeted at several types of groups including those who sided with the Royalists during the English Civil War; those who had fought against Cromwell; those who stood in the way of the seizing of land to pay Cromwellian troops and officers; and finally a catch-all group: 'all Irish Catholics who had taken no part in the war of 1649-52, but had remained quiet, were again liable to be transplanted, unless they had manifested a constant good affection in favour of the Parliament and against the King'.[25] If, as suggested, Spike Island was used as a holding area for those bound for transplantation in the late 1640s, it was to set a trend for the island, which was later involved in the practice of sending felons to Australia.

Star-shaped Fortress

The French Revolution began in 1789 and by 1791 Britain found herself officially at war with France. This, together with Britain's defeat in the American Revolution in 1781, would have led her military strategists to anticipate a new hostile foe on her western seaboard. It is not surprising then that the military fortifications were upgraded in Cork Harbour at this time. From 1792 the building of Fort Westmoreland on Spike Island commenced. The older forts of Camden and Carlisle were also upgraded. Forced convict labour was to be a feature of ongoing works and it is estimated that 400 to 500 convicts were used.

This use of convicts as an unpaid labour source had been widespread from the very beginnings of transportation. In the eighteenth century, convicts, regardless of where they were being sent, were either assigned to colonial settlers for use as agricultural workers or were assigned as 'government men'. In both America and Australia, where convicts were sent, they could be given to landowners to use as they saw fit, as farm labourers or servants. There was no real responsibility on the part of the landowner to do anything for the convict other than to clothe and feed them. This arrangement could last for the duration of the convict's sentence, which was typically seven to fourteen years. Those assigned as 'government men' were accommodated in barrack-type buildings and used by the colonial administration as a labour force to build roads, bridges, municipal buildings and in some cases, fortresses. Having convicts work on the upgrading of the Cork Harbour forts was not out of the ordinary.

In addition to the building of Fort Westmoreland on Spike, extensive landscaping had to be undertaken to prepare a flat circular base from which the artillery could command an imposing position over the entrance of the harbour. This almost symmetric shape remains clearly visible today. In 1805 the victualling station of the Royal Navy moved from Kinsale to Haulbowline Island. Again, convicts were used to build new store-houses and infrastructure. At this time a causeway was built between Spike and Haulbowline Island, the remains of which can still be seen at low tide. It extends from the south-eastern side of Haulbowline towards neighbouring Spike and a small upright perch marks its presence when the tide causes it to be submerged. Looking out from Cobh this causeway between the two islands would have been clearly visible at the time of its completion.

The use of convicts for slave labour, and indeed the entire system of transportation, did however come under scrutiny from various elements of society and eventually from political quarters. Transportation as a form of punishment began to be reconsidered in the late 1840s and early 1850s. In 1847 Spike Island was opened as a penal station and operated as such until 1883. Coleman states that 2,500 were stationed there in 1850.[26]

Although nothing on the scale of this transplanta-tion had occurred in Ireland before, the idea of transposing those thought of as problem citizens was not new. In the past, people who found themselves on the wrong side of the authorities had been sent to various British colonies. This system, as I have mentioned, was known as transportation. In the beginning transportation was used as an alternative to hanging for capital offences. Rather than a criminal being put on the end of a rope, they were sent away and used for the good of the emerging empire. This facilitated claims that the concept of transportation was a humane one. While this may have been arguable in the case of death sentences, the later practice of imposing long sentences of transportation for minor crimes reduced the force of the argument. As time went on, the number of offences that resulted in transportation increased and finally included some very minor crimes indeed. There were sentences of transportation for stealing, being drunk and disorderly and for vagrancy. The use of this system for even petty crimes was to have an adverse effect on those who later found themselves at variance with the law during the famine, when the stealing of a loaf of bread to feed hungry children could result in a sentence of seven or fourteen years in a hostile environment on the far side of the world.

5

Transportation and the Convicts of Cork Harbour

From the late eighteenth century, Cork Harbour became one of the two main embarkation points in Ireland for the transport vessels that conveyed convicts to Australia and Van Diemen's Land. Dublin was the second.

People throughout Ireland who were sentenced to transportation in their local jurisdictions had to be initially conveyed to a port of embarkation. Having been held in bridewells and local gaols around the country, convicts were often marched on foot from as far away as Limerick to be incarcerated in the gaols in and around Cork City, to await transportation. They stayed in these institutions while the necessary logistical arrangements were made for their passage to Australia. In the county and city gaols, those from outside County Cork were known to the other inmates as 'foreigners'. Over time, however, it was Cork Harbour that came to be the place where convicts awaited their fate. Initially this was to be on-board a prison hulk, and later, as the practice of transportation was being discontinued, on Spike Island in the lower harbour. Although physically more convenient for the loading of the transport ships, Cork Harbour did not originally have any holding centres for the convicts, apart from one four-person bridewell in Cobh.[27]

Why then, when there was already a city and county gaol operational in nearby Cork, did the harbour become the place of incarceration for convicts? This move raises several questions; what happened to these convicts on Spike Island? And were there other places in the harbour that 'hosted' convicts?

The history of transportation traces its origins from the late sixteenth century. From this period onwards numerous laws were passed in Britain that facilitated the sending of felons abroad. In 1597 the '*Acte for the punyshment of rogues, vagabonds and sturdy beggars*' was passed, which provided for such people to be sent 'out of this realm … and conveyed unto such parts beyond the seas and as shall be at any time hereafter assyned for that purpose by the Privy Council…'[28] Although originally intended to rid the streets of the criminal element, it was conceded quite early that the convicts could be used as a labour force, which was to become particularly useful in the imperial endeavour to build up distant colonies. The Transportation Act of 1717 makes reference to this usage, 'In many of His Majesty's colonies and plantations in America, there was a great want of servants, who by their labour and industry might be the means of improving and making the said colonies and plantations more useful to this nation.'[29]

During the seventeenth century, convicts were sent to the fledgling new British colonies in places like Virginia and Massachusetts. In 1649 and 1650, Cromwell 'banished' Irishmen he claimed were involved in the rebellion to the Caribbean for use on plantations there in what was described as 'transplantation'.[30]

Loss of Colonies

One of the consequences of Britain's loss of colonies in the War of Independence was the discontinuing of sending convicts to America. Up to 1776, convicts had been transported there and used as a labour force either to undertake government infrastructural building or to assist the colonists themselves on their farms and plantations. With the loss of the American colonies, pressure was growing on the penal system in Britain to accommodate the large number of convicts and in 1787, what became known as the 'First Fleet' left England to set sail for Australia.

In addition to the colonists on board the 11 ships,

there were 548 male and 188 female convicts. In 1788 Britain officially announced that Australia was to be the new penal colony. Over the following 80 years somewhere in the region of 160,000 convicts[31] were transported from Great Britain and Ireland to Australia and, from 1805, Van Diemen's Land (now Tasmania). Of this number, 30,000 men and 9,000 women and children were sent from Cork Harbour. Once convicted and sentenced to transportation, convicts were held in local gaols, holding centres or on the prison hulks anchored in Cork Harbour. They would be held in these places until their numbers were sufficient to justify the leasing of a 'transport' vessel to take them to Australia or Van Diemen's Land. During this waiting period, convicts were used as a labour force to carry out municipal and military works for the government.

Transportation to the American colonies was discontinued following the Declaration of Independence and the ensuing conflict, which made it impractical and unwise to send convicts there. With this outlet for undesirables closed off, the gaols and prisons of Great Britain and Ireland strained under increasing numbers. Believing the inconvenience would be only temporary and the rebels soon defeated, Britain contrived a temporary solution to the problem of overcrowded gaols at home by the utilisation of prison hulks. These decommissioned naval vessels could be used as holding places until transportation resumed to America, or other locations were found. The latter became necessary when Britain surrendered in 1781, following their defeat at the hands of the rebels in Yorktown, Virginia, in the closing chapter of the War of Independence. The hulks, which were originally intended to be a stop gap measure, became a more permanent feature, and pressure mounted to find an alternative destination where the labour of these felons could be put to good use in the service of the empire.

Botany Bay

Although Botany Bay had been discovered, named and recommended as a suitable location for colonisation by Captain Cook, it was found unsuitable by the first fleet. In search of a better location, they sailed up the coast and chose a large natural harbour that they named Sydney Cove. This was to become the first penal colony of Australia and over the ensuing seventy years approximately 168,000 men, women and children were to be sent there, and to numerous other locations on the continent of what is known today as Australasia. Of these, almost 25 per cent were Irish, most of whom had embarked from Dublin and Cork. In its first three years as a penal colony, New South Wales received no convict ships from Ireland. This was due to a legislative deficiency that did not provide for transportation from Ireland to anywhere other that Europe and America. This matter was resolved by a new Act passed in 1790 (30 Geo. III c32)[32], which paved the way for the first convicts from Ireland to that destination.

There has been a tendency in some quarters to associate the majority of Irish convicts sent to Australia with crimes relating to the struggle for independence. In fact, the range of crimes for which one could be transported varied immensely. In a number of cases a sentence of death was converted to transportation, but the death sentence was applicable to many crimes some of which would not seem to merit such a harsh response. In many instances the crimes were petty in nature, like housebreaking, stealing and desertion from the army.

Apart from in Dublin, Ireland lacked the indigenous urban crime associated with cities like London, and therefore many of the crimes were wrought of a rural environment. The stealing of pigs, sheep and horses featured heavily in the accounts of offences. In times of hardship, such as the crop failures and famine of the mid-nineteenth century, it was inevitable that stealing food would find many individuals brought before the so-called 'assizes', which were the sessions of the principal courts in each county. Others found themselves there as a result of clashes between landlords and tenant groups. Although there has been a tendency to assume that a large number of convicts were convicted for rebellious activities, Professor Shaw maintains that there was probably no more than 600 of the 30,000 transported that had been sentenced for rebellion.[33]

Whatever the offence, when the sentence of transportation had been handed down, the convicts were assembled and brought to the Cork county or city gaols. In the case of Cork, the city gaol was located on North Gate Bridge; in 1807 this was described as 'very old and dilapidated but well run'.[34] There were plans at that stage to build a new gaol, but criticism emerged due to the inordinate delay. Convicts were detained in both gaols until the necessary transport ships were sourced by the government and made ready to convey them to Australia or Van Diemen's Land.

During their 'stay' at these prisons, convicts awaiting transportation were allocated 1s 1d per day to facilitate the expense of food and accommodation. When a transport ship was ready, the convicts would be brought downriver from Cork City to the lower harbour to board the waiting vessels.

It was this distribution of allowance by the prison warders and the arrangements for the delivery of convicts to the transport ships, which hold the key to the emergence of Cork Harbour as the location for the actual holding of convicts. Up to 1822, convicts destined for Australia would be sent to and incarcerated in these county and city gaols of Cork. It was very often days or weeks before a transport ship became available to take them but the warders didn't mind, as keeping the convicts was healthy a source of income. The 13*d* per day given to the warder was meant to pay for the keep of the convict, but in the early nineteenth century allegations of abuse were brought to the attention of the authorities. A commission was established to look into the matter and in a report and the minutes of evidence were delivered in March 1817. The investigative team visited Cove to board a number of transport ships that were about to set sail for New South Wales. They interviewed several convicts, who claimed that they had only received 6*d* per day from the warder, which they were told was their allowance to purchase food. Other abuses also came to light; it was discovered that the turnkey in Cork was controlling and profiting from the sale of alcohol in the prison.

Equally serious was the discovery that warders were deliberately delaying convict's transfers onto the transport ships. This was so that they could continue their profiteering and collect the daily allowances of the convicts. Questions were asked as to why people were kept in the crowded county gaols when the ships had been made ready. The warder was told he was in breach of a parliamentary act in retaining any part of an allowance in lieu of feeding the prisoners under his jurisdiction. It was also revealed that the warder was not living on the prison. The commission of inquiry also reported on some deplorable conditions on one particular vessel that had left Dublin on 30 January. On 9 February, the vessel still had female convicts on board, held in appalling conditions; there were sixty-three confined to a space 22ft by 16 ft.[35]

These outrages and others like them prompted the government to look at improving conditions and also saving money. Several further inspections took place, but in 1822 it was decided to adopt the practice of using hulks in Cork. Thus the scandals of conditions in city establishments, as well as financial and other abuses, contributed to the harbour becoming a place of waiting, not just an embarkation point.

As previously mentioned, the use of decommissioned naval ships had begun when the outlet for transportation of convicts to the American colonies had ceased. These ships were unseaworthy and had been placed at anchor on the Thames and in other estuaries in Britain to serve as holding prisons. It was initially thought to be a temporary measure. Britain believed that there would be a speedy victory over the colonials in America but it was of course the British who conceded defeat in Yorktown in 1781. The new political reality of an independent America meant Britain lost, among other things, a destination for her convicts; in the preceding fifty years about 30,000 convicts had been transported to these American colonies.[36] The gaols in Britain became overcrowded and the 'temporary' use of the hulks became a more permanent feature of the system, even after the announcement in 1788 of a new penal colony in New South Wales. Neither the hulks nor the convict depots, where the felons were assembled prior to transportation, had ever been intended for use as places of permanent incarceration, but that is what happened. McConville suggests that 'the convict prisons, which had grown out of a problem with the transportation of convicts overseas, eventually replaced transportation altogether'.[37] The deployment of Spike Island and the hulks in Cork Harbour would later emerge from these developments in the British penal system.

In 1823, the hulk *Surprise* arrived at Cork Harbour. Over the next eleven years it served as a holding vessel for convicts awaiting transportation to Australia. Official reports by inspectors each year praised the conditions on board as being very good. During the period of its use in the harbour, 5,467 convicts were transported from the vessel to New South Wales, with an average of 148 prisoners aboard on any given day. Altogether there were five escapes and forty-four deaths on board during this period.

The running of the hulk was overseen by twelve people, only two of whom lived on board; a keeper and a ship keeper, who received £200 and £100 respectively per year. The remainder of the crew consisted of a local inspector, who was paid £250 per year; six sailors, who were paid £20 annually; and for the physical and moral welfare of the convicts, a visiting surgeon was paid £150 and Catholic and Protestant chaplains were each paid £50.[38] The vessel lay off Haulbowline and its appointed superintendent was a Mr Trevor, with a Mr Hollingsworth holding the appointment of inspector.[39]

As Victorian attitudes changed about how prisons should be run, significant developments in Britain led to the state itself becoming involved in the running and administration of convict prisons. New concepts regarding the reform of criminals began to be reflected in government policy. For centuries, gaols and houses of correction had maintained a narrow function as holding centres for debtors or those awaiting charges or sentences. Detention in its own right was not widely imposed or deemed a punishment; it was only introduced as such in 1811.[40] Until this time the methodology for the control of crime was the use of a system of corporal and capital punishments; monetary fines, the physical whipping of felons, even hanging.

In 1842 the British Government built and operated its own penitentiary at Pentonville. The prison was built with the new philosophy of reform in mind. This had been adopted following a detailed study and report in 1838 and the approach that was to be taken included three stages. In the first of these a system of 'separate' confinement was imposed. This incorporated a revolutionary idea of having one prisoner per cell. They were to be kept in this type of solitary confinement for eighteen months before being transported. It was believed that this separation would prevent the worst effects of convicts mixing with each other and learning further criminality, and would also be a mechanism to 'break' the spirit so that one could be more readily directed to resume a better life. Convicts who conformed were given early 'tickets of leave' on reaching Australia. By 1853, legislation had been enacted to commute sentences of transportation to that of penal servitude.[41] Incentives by way of scoring points to reduce the length of the sentence were balanced by physical punishments that could be imposed for poor behaviour. Work and hard labour were an integral part of this system of reform.[42]

In 1845 the Inspector General's report for Ireland related proudly that the government's building plan for the upgrading of all prisons had been progressing very well with only three counties left where a first class prison was yet to be built.[43] There were enough well-built prisons now to tackle any overcrowding and provide for the needs of prisoner space and exercise yards consistent with the new approaches in penitential policy. It seemed that the Irish penal system was destined to follow the path of the English one, but this was not to be the case. Like all other aspects of Irish life, the catastrophic events of the Great Famine were to be reflected in the gaols and houses of detention. Spike Island was to become a central player in the judicial system's response to these events.

6

The Great Famine
and Spike Island

The recurrent crop failures brought about by the potato blight in Ireland from late 1845 through to 1852, coupled with an inadequate British Government response, reluctant to provide aid, resulted in a famine of epic proportions. The high dependency of the population on the potato as a food source was to have catastrophic consequences on the largely agricultural population of the country. Ireland before the famine had a population of over eight million people. In its aftermath there was only six million. Two million people were gone; about half of these were lost to emigration, the remainder to disease and starvation. One million people died.[44]

It is difficult today to comprehend the scale of this disaster. In December 2004 a tsunami in the Indian Ocean caused the deaths of over 220,000 people. The casualties were stretched across a vast geographical spread affecting numerous countries but mainly

Indonesia, Sri Lanka, India and Thailand. There were also casualties as far apart as Tanzania and Bangladesh. The extensive television images of the destruction and the human cost were horrific. It seemed that there were dead bodies everywhere. If one considers, then, the million or more who died in Ireland during the years of the famine, in such a comparatively small geographical location, it is almost incomprehensible. Many have asked how such a catastrophe could occur in the first place, not to mention why measures were not immediately put in place to relieve the distress and curb the huge mortality rate that decimated whole families and communities. The answers to these questions are varied, complex and beyond the scope of this book. Nevertheless, given that crop failure, food shortages and the administrative and relief responses all directly impacted on the utilisation of Spike Island, it is useful to at least identify some of the circumstances of the darkest period of Ireland's history.

The potato blight was a destructive fungus properly known as *Phytophthora infestans*. The first indication of a problem was the appearance of distinctive black spots on the leaves of the crop as the damp weather facilitated the potency of the fungus. Spread of the fungus was rapid and resulted in the potatoes turning to a black stinking mush. In the case of the Great Famine, it initially reached Ireland in late 1845. One third of the crop was lost and it worsened the following year.[45]

Given that two thirds of the country was dependent on agriculture at that time, the stage was set for major difficulties.[46] People across the country did not have the luxury of going to work every day in a factory and receiving regular payment, as was the case in many of the emerging industrial economies in Britain and elsewhere. Many tenant farmers sublet small parcels of land to labourers whose only pay was the capacity to grow their own food. Given the potato's ability to produce far more nutrition per square metre of ground than, say, a grain crop, it was therefore better suited as a food source for people with very small holdings. The main problem at this point, then, was that for many people living on such land, the potato had become their only nourishment. The average consumption of potatoes per person per day in Ireland was much higher than other European averages. A plateful of potatoes mixed with buttermilk or, on special occasions, some meat, was the normal day to day diet of millions. Numerous widespread crop failures exacerbated the shortages of supply. Potatoes that had been set aside for animal feed and for seeding for the next crop were used for human consumption. One of the biggest problems was that even in a good year, potatoes as a product could not be stored indefinitely.

In times of scarcity food prices also rose sharply and the stage was set for further suffering as the potato blight wrought havoc with crops all over the country.

As each month passed, it seemed an indifferent British Government was far more intent on complying with the principals of political economy, than with meaningfully tackling the difficulties that were about to give rise to human suffering.

As food shortages gripped the country, families sought ways of getting food from labouring, from relief work where it was available and eventually by begging or even stealing. Those who had the money to do so emigrated. They fled not just the prospect of starvation but the threat of infectious diseases. At that time there was no real understanding of how disease was transmitted and in many instances fleeing on cramped vessels to North America and Canada put people in the way of infection. At an island called Grosse Île (in the St Lawrence Seaway) a quarantine station for immigrants into Canada checked people coming ashore for disease by various means, including placing a spatula on their tongues to check for infection. The problem was that the same spatula was used for the next person in line, causing cross-infection in otherwise healthy people.

There are many written accounts of dreadful conditions regarding ships arriving from Ireland in 1847. In early May 1847, 200 beds for the sick were deemed sufficient on Grosse Île by the doctor in charge there. There had never been more than one hundred sick patients on the island at any one time prior to this.

By 19 May, 258 sick people had been taken off ships coming from Ireland. Five days later there was another 500 sick on ships. By the end of May the island was witnessing fifty to sixty deaths per day. In 1847, out of a total of 398 ships that were inspected at Grosse Île, 157 were from Ireland, this being the highest proportion of the ports of origin.[47] These figures and conditions serve to highlight the desperate attempts of people in Ireland to flee the ravages of disease and hunger.

The effects of the famine on social norms were also striking. The plight of people caught up in the famine was horrendous and social order often broke down. Threats were issued by famished tenants against landlords, people were driven to steal food or livestock and fighting often broke out among those searching for sustenance. Liam Kennedy suggests that one could think of the famine as 'an example, albeit an extreme one, of a socially disruptive force that uprooted individuals and their families and in the process weakened or destroyed existing social norms'.[48]

Admissions to existing gaols inevitably reflected the social upheaval caused by widespread disease and hunger. Up to 1846, the prison system was thought to have been more than adequate for the number of felons and debtors going through the courts and assizes. There had been a countrywide policy to update and improve accommodation in gaols in line with new thinking in prison reform. However, in 1847 the prison system in

Ireland became completely overwhelmed. The report of the inspector general commences:

> No task can be well more discouraging and indeed melancholy than that of attempting to detail the history of Irish prisons for the year of 1847. Our predecessors … brought the county gaols, as a general rule, to a state of which any country could be proud … when the terrible catastrophe, which has disorganised the whole framework of society in Ireland, fell with its full force upon the establishments under our charge; and instead of having a pleasing statement of improved discipline, enlarged prison accommodation and advanced instruction, we can only describe industrial works given up, classification destroyed, separation unattempted and disease and death increasing to a degree that could never have been contemplated by those acquainted with the usual orderly and healthy state of our gaols.[49]

His observations of that year still resound powerfully over one-and-a-half centuries later. The Inspector General attributes the calamity befalling the prison service to three principal reasons: firstly, the famine; secondly, the cessation of the transportation of convicts to Van Diemen's Land[50]; and lastly the introduction of the Vagrancy Act. The two judicial measures, combined with the catastrophic effects of the famine in Ireland, resulted in increased admissions to prisons.

The famine had resulted in mass movements of people from place to place. Their mobilisation was precipitated by a number of factors. People moved in search for food. When crops failed in a locality they set out from their immediate area and went further afield to secure supplies. In some instances they may have thought that the potato blight did not extend beyond a couple of miles. Communications and mass media were not like those of today and not knowing whether a neighbouring village or county was affected by the crop failure resulted in people travelling the surrounding countryside. For many, their efforts were in vain. In the early stages, as shortages of food gripped the country, supplies could be obtained, but for ever increasing prices. When even the meagre supplies available went beyond the reach of the poorer classes, many were reduced to scouring the earth in search of anything that could be eaten; roaming from village to village and farm to farm, in an endless search for sustenance. Horrific eyewitness accounts of the period relate skeletal-like frames, endlessly walking the countryside until they could walk no further, finally lying down to die with the telling green stains around their mouths, having eaten grass in a desperate attempt to survive.

With the effects of starvation and social impoverishment came disease. More people died in the famine from disease than from starvation. In many cases the onset and rapid spread of the diseases that accompany famine resulted in whole communities fleeing in terror. There was no understanding at that time of how germs and viruses were spread.

Crop failures and food shortages were not uncommon in Ireland. There had, in the past, been many similar problems associated with the agricultural way of life. In most decades from the 1700s to the 1840s there had been reports of famine and severe hardship, but nothing before or since came close to the sheer scale of suffering, disease and death throughout most of Ireland in the years between 1845 and 1852.

A major problem at the time was that the British government had a firmly entrenched belief in the doctrine of political economy and laissez-faire. This economic doctrine preached that the market should not be interfered with, and that the provision of aid could have a long-term detrimental effect on the morality of the population. They feared that people who became accustomed to handouts would be morally corrupted. It was believed that such activity would make them forever dependent and take away any incentive to work for themselves. Aid should only be granted in the most destitute of circumstances and even then it was to be tightly controlled and not subject to perceived abuses.

Eventually, when confronted with one of the greatest humanitarian catastrophes ever witnessed in peacetime Europe, they moved to provide assistance; the decision was made to have local landlords meet the costs. This was to be done by taxing them according to the number of tenants they had on their land. Many landlords were helpful and willingly joined relief committees. Others however, who were being taxed heavily to finance relief schemes, evicted families to reduce their rateable taxes. This left whole families not just homeless, but without the plot of land that was the only means they had to feed their families. The number of those evicted is difficult to determine; past estimates have varied between 70,000 families and 500,000 people.[51] Wherever the true figure may lie, the spread of infectious disease was facilitated greatly by the situation of homelessness.

Two of the main killers of the famine, typhus and relapsing fever are spread by the human louse. They both have slightly different methods of transmission but the possibility of louse infestation where people were reduced to living on the side of the road or in hastily made shacks in ditches, only served to hasten their susceptibility to fever. Overcrowded prison cells were to pose the same inherent dangers to health. The deadly cycle of nutritional deprivation followed by eviction and infestation was now exacerbated by the introduction of the Vagrancy Act in 1847.[52] This Act made it a felony for a person to desert or leave their dependent wives or children for the purpose of becoming eligible for aid from the state, either inside or outside the workhouses. The emphasis here was the 'criminality' not of abandoning your family, but of leaving the state in a position where they would have to provide aid. This one Act alone gives an indication of the thinking of the day regarding the assistance of the deprived. It was a crime to leave your family in such a position that the state may have to look after them. Yet the system of transportation created the very same situation.

It is interesting to compare this approach in light of the effects of transportation. Many men were forced to 'abandon' their families by a harsh judicial system that sent them to the other side of the world for protracted periods, often for very minor offences. During the famine there were many instances of people being transported for seven years for stealing food. In a situation where they could no longer provide for their families because of the lack of work and food it was case of having very few choices. If a father left his family with the intention of them finding themselves 'in the care of the state' he was guilty of a crime. If, in desperation, he stole food for them, he was also considered a criminal. The judicial workings of the state in such cases surely facilitated destitution rather than prevented it.

The Vagrancy Act also made it an offence for 'every person wandering abroad and begging, or placing himself in any public place, highway, public court or passage to beg or gather alms'.[53] Under this provision, people who found themselves literally begging for food or aid anywhere in public were committing an offence. Given the fear of disease and the evictions of huge numbers of people onto the public roads, many were now in breach of the Vagrancy Act and were therefore liable to prosecution and incarceration. Initially, a conviction for vagrancy was not supposed to be punishable by transportation, rather imprisonment and hard labour was recommended. Nevertheless, many of the 'convicts' on Spike Island were under sentence of transportation for such offences.[54]

This legislation criminalised people who were in fact victims of the famine. In many instances it was circumstances beyond their control that led them to be in breach of the law. What parent or brother with no home, means of employment, money or food would not beg or even steal to feed his starving children or dependents? An examination of the 'offences' of the convict population at Spike Island during the years of the famine reveals many instances of stealing food, produce or livestock.

John Ahern of Co. Kerry ended up on Spike Island having being convicted of cow stealing in January 1847. He had received a sentence of seven years' transportation.[55]

In November 1847, Joseph Connell was sent to Spike Island to await transportation for seven years for the crime of 'stealing potatoes'.[56] The stealing of potatoes was hardly the activity of a master criminal. There is surely only one reason a person would steal potatoes, to feed themselves or their families.

When Patrick Croke was caught 'killing a sheep with intent', he received seven years' transportation and he too found himself on Spike Island.[57] This strange description of his offence probably defines the desperation of the period. What was his intention? To stuff the sheep and place it over his mantelpiece? Or, as is most probably the case, to slaughter for consumption.

Michael McGurk never left Spike. He died there in 1852 having been originally convicted for 'stealing cereal articles' in July 1849.[58]

John Morgan from Drogheda was sixty years old. He was married with two children and was sentenced to seven years' transportation for stealing four chickens. He died, still a prisoner in Port Arthur, Tasmania at the age of eighty-four having never been reunited with his family.

Thomas Cahill from Co. Tipperary was only twelve years old when he was transported for seven years for vagrancy. Because of his age he was sent to Point Puer. An island prison for boys off Port Arthur, Point Puer was infamous for the number of suicides of young inmates there.

At the age of thirteen, William Mulhall got seven years' transportation for stealing a pair of shoes. Towards the end of his sentence he was further charged with the offence of smoking tobacco and for this his sentence was extended. In his despair he tried to hang himself. This too was deemed an offence and he was sentenced to suffer more years in the system that was transportation.

The mitigating circumstances of these 'crimes' did not prevent the system from immediately categorising the perpetrators as criminals. The question must be raised as to whether their situation, or more pointedly the situation of their families, was made worse by a system that took little account of the unfolding catastrophe of the time. A man forced to watch his family slowly starving, compelled by the instinct of protection and survival, will seek food from any source. He will beg, borrow or steal to prevent the agonising effects of starvation. If caught in these acts he will go before a court and be sentenced to seven or fourteen years' transportation. What happens to the family? The fear of impending destitution led many families to appeal for clemency at the assizes and, if unsuccessful, for permission to travel to Australia with their men.

Was Spike Island a depot for malicious, ill-intentioned criminals? Certainly there were some such people there, but many were those who stole to eat. The killing of a sheep 'with intent' surely meant the intent to eat it. If this is the case, and it was induced by starvation, was seven years' transportation fair?

As noted by the prison authorities themselves, the admission rate to gaols had quadrupled in the years leading up to 1847. By their own admission there is a direct link between the catastrophe of the famine and the upsurge in demand on prison spaces. The quadrupling of convictions meant there was insufficient accommodation in all the gaols of the country.

Another compelling problem was that the law now dictated that a cell was to contain no more than one man; but it could not now have fewer than three.[59] This meant that cells built for one had to now accommodate at least three. In fact, people ended up lying in hallways, day rooms and any available space, all contributing to the calamity. Undoubtedly these cramped conditions facilitated the transfer of infectious diseases. In Cork county gaol, prison deaths had numbered just two in 1816, twelve in 1846, and one year later, in 1847, 351 convicts died. Overall, the first year of the famine saw a tenfold increase in the mortality rate within the Irish prison system, rising from 131 deaths the year before, to a staggering 1,315.[60]

The main killer diseases of the period were typhus, cholera, relapsing fever, smallpox and dysentery.[61] The new, cramped conditions of the prisons were a veritable breeding ground for these very often fatal diseases. The fourfold increase in persons being convicted placed enormous pressure on gaols all over the country. There was simply no way in which the current system could accommodate the new 'famine felons'.

Such was the background to the opening of Spike Island as a convict depot on 9 October 1847. 600 spaces for convicts had been created with an immediate intention to upgrade to 800. The idea was not a new one; Spike had first been mentioned as a possible place of detention as early as 1835. A number of modifications were undertaken on the island to accommodate the first 600 convicts but this was later increased to 1,500. Spike Island, in the middle of Cork Harbour, became the second location for the placement of convicts. It operated as a convict depot until the cessation of transportation altogether, but was to continue as a penal colony until its convicts were transferred to Dublin in 1883.

The initial convicts on Spike were incarcerated during the Great Famine and were among those referred to by the Inspector General. Many of them would have found themselves, by circumstances beyond their control, to be in breach of the law. Apart from the starvation, which led many people to steal food and farm produce including pigs, sheep and cattle, people also found themselves wandering from one locality to another in search of food. Felonies such as the stealing of livestock, food and provisions all attracted sentences of transportation and many of those convicted of such offences ended up on Spike.

The immovable doctrine of laissez-faire observed by the British Government of the day prevented intervention in the practice of widespread evictions. The Vagrancy Act criminalised poverty-stricken people caught up in the maelstrom of starvation and disease.

The workhouse system, which barely provided enough sustenance to keep people alive, was vacated by many, who deliberately put themselves in the way of the law in order to get imprisoned as they thought the ration of food superior. The combination of these policies and the calamity of the famine filled Spike Island to capacity and beyond.

During the period of incarceration on Spike Island, the number of convicts who died there was often proportionally higher than any other prison in Ireland. In 1854 one of the worst mortality rates was recorded, with 238 convicts dying on the island that year.[62] This represented 11 per cent of the convict population, while other convict depots such as Newgate, Smithfield and Mountjoy had mortality rates of 6 per cent, 5 per cent and 2 per cent respectively. Other years, mortality rates were always in the high 30s and 50s for a prison population of just over 2,000. Official reports cite several reasons for the higher than usual rates on Spike Island. These include the prevailing winds and bad weather, which the medical officer claimed, when coupled with poor sewage and inadequate hospital facilities, was the reason for these deaths.

Another explanation offered by the authorities on Spike was that many prisoners coming from county gaols were already suffering from the conditions that resulted in their deaths on the island. The outside labour undertaken by these men, in the public works and upkeep works on the fort, are never cited as having anything to do with the health and welfare of the men. In fact many reports complain that the convicts on Spike were not subjected to sufficient punishment. This seems strange on reading the instructions given by the Inspector General to the governor of the convict depot when it first opened.

The Work Ethic on Spike

Inspector General Clement Johnson set out very clearly that this establishment was to be penal in nature. In a letter to the governor of Spike Island he reminded him that Spike Island, being only a temporary arrangement, would not resort to the usual methods of punishment enjoyed by institutions that had been built and equipped specifically for the purpose of criminal reform. Therefore, he argued, a specific type of management would be necessary there. Among the measures he recommended were 'ceaseless supervision and vigilance combined with a strict course of firmness' and that convicts be 'constantly employed under strict inspection'. Concerned that the accommodation for convicts was in thirty-man dormitories, which was not consistent with 'separate' policy, it was suggested that by bedtime convicts should be too exhausted to do anything other than sleep. He points out that the interior of the fort is unlevelled, with large protruding rocks impeding communication. Convicts were to be utilised in levelling the entire interior. His instructions are quite specific regarding the ethos that this establishment must adopt:

> I now approach a point which I wish most especially to impress upon your mind – I mean the fact that Spike Island is *penal* in its nature and that, although every attention must be paid to the health of the prisoners and to that *degree of comfort upon which health depends*, it is by no means our wish that it should be made a desirable residence, or that the position of the convicts should be on a level with, not to say superior to, that of the industrious labourer outside. For this purpose the labour extracted from them must, as far as possible, be continuous and severe.[63]

The inspector emphasised that those on Spike Island were to be no better off than if they were sent to Van Diemen's Land. Visitors were expressly forbidden, as were letters to and from loved ones. Military officers were to be sent to Spike to train the turnkeys in using a particular type of hard labour as punishment. No books were to be permitted.

Certainly from 1847 to 1852, during the worst ravages of the Great Famine, the easy transmission of disease coupled with the increased numbers of those incarcerated would have added to the morality rate. But what of the years that followed? Many died in the 1860s; men of eighteen, nineteen and twenty.

A contributing factor may have been the reform practices that had been implemented by Victorian penitential policy. Harsh attitudes in relation to food, hard labour and strict discipline took its toll among the prison population.

Spike opened as place of confinement during the worst possible confluence of events for those who found themselves caught up in the penitential system. It was during this period that attitudes to confinement and forced reform were to result in an ever harsher regime.

When overcrowding was at its worst in the country's prisons and depots, Spike Island was increasingly used as an overspill for excess elsewhere in the country. Other forts in the harbour saw the arrival of criminals; in April 1850, Fort Camden and Carlisle saw 81 and 120 convicts respectively assigned to them. Although the prisoners, for administration purposes, remained under the jurisdiction of Spike Island, they were accommodated in these forts and used as labour for upgrading and maintaining the defences of the harbour. Thus, across the years of transportation from 1792 to 1867, Cork Harbour had become the place of incarceration for thousands of convicts with Spike at its centre. Many believing they were destined for colonies around the world went no further than Cork Harbour.

Irish National archives list 757 convicts who died on Spike Island. The records do not show any detailed causes of death. It was unusual for any reasons to be proffered to family or kin when a convict died. In the vast majority of cases, no headstone was erected either. It was the final indignity for convicts; unmarked graves in unhallowed ground. This was true of both Spike Island and other more distant penal stations.

One of the most dreaded convict destinations in Australia was Van Diemen's Land (VDL). Later known as Tasmania, Australia's only island state. Although named by a Dutch captain after the owner of his shipping company, the name in English had a 'demonic' ring to it. Convicts who went to there were processed in the same way as at other penal colonies and used for either government building programmes or for extra cheap labour for colonists. If a convict committed a second offence while in VDL they would be punished by being sent to Port Arthur. At Port Arthur, as at Spike, those who died received little ceremony. A small island just off the penal station was used to bury convicts and for that reason became known as the Isle of the Dead. On this island there are fewer than twenty convict headstones, despite the burial of over 1,769.[64] It seems only convicts who became highly regarded or very trusted were eventually afforded the dignity of a headstone.

On Spike it seems similar practices prevailed. The burial site for convicts was on the western side of the island. On the centenary of the famine in 1947 an area there was walled off with a Celtic cross erected to commemorate those who had died on the island while it was a penal station. This is a 'representative' cemetery and does not encompass the entire burial area used for interring convicts. Burial sites for individuals, although in a general area, were random and remain unmarked. A hole was dug, the body placed in it and the hole covered over. Only a tiny percentage did get a headstone (of which only about twelve remain on Spike Island), and these individuals only had their initials, the date and a prisoner number etched on them.

Questions remain regarding the cause of the deaths of those convicts on Spike. Some of those listed as having died were as young as fifteen. Despite the fact that some of these deaths must have been attributable to malnutrition and disease from the famine in the late 1840s, the figure of 757 people who did not survive their incarceration on Spike Island over a thirty-six year period is still alarmingly high and besides. not all of the deaths took place in the 1840s. It is difficult to conciliate these figures to the description of conditions related by the Spike Island Presbyterian Chaplain Revd C.B. Gibson, who related, 'The prisoners are fairly fed and fairly worked; and when they leave prison they are generally better able to do a fair day's work than when they entered it.'[65]

These remarks, quoted in 1893, are very similar to remarks the author heard on a guided tour of Port Arthur in 2002. The conditions under which convicts were held were presented as being mildly uncomfortable but better than what they would be accustomed to at home. There seemed to have been very little consideration given to the hardship inflicted on remaining family members by the process of separation and transportation. Little information is offered on the causes of death or on the relative cruelty and hardship inflicted on people who, in many instances, were guilty of very petty crimes. The only conviction referred to by John Coleman in his *Story of Spike Island* is that of a Dr William Burke Kirwan who murdered his wife and 'got away with' penal servitude for life.[66] But even a cursory look at the records of convictions reveals a selection of seven year sentences and more for crimes such as pig stealing, vagrancy and drunkenness.

Convict transportation was a harsh and difficult punishment. It often ruined whole families where the main breadwinner disappeared into the system when sent to the far side of the world. Wives and children left to fend for themselves often pleaded with judges to be allowed to travel with their convicted husbands, for fear of being left at home with no support and in a position where only stealing, begging or prostitution would ensure survival. For the convicts who were finally placed on the transports, life was not good either. If a convict survived the hulks and the hard labour, they were eventually placed on the transport ships that were anchored and waiting in the harbour. Dark holds were filled to capacity with chained bodies. There was no lighting or sanitation facilities, and when all were aboard the holds were battened down. Below, terrified convicts, many of whom had never been to sea, only knew their voyage had begun when the darkened interior began to rise and fall with the motion of the sea. Ships like the *Britannia*, which, sailing from Cork to Sydney in 1796, was recorded as being one of the most depraved, brutal and cruellest voyages ever undertaken. Disease, torture, starvation and cruelty resulted in the deaths of one in every six men onboard.

The thousands who left these shores in chains to one final, longing look at the rolling hills and wooded headlands of Cork Harbour before being shoved below deck on the transportation ship, into the squalid surroundings that would be their hell for the next few months. They ached at the prospect of separation and departure. The next hills they would see would be in Sydney Cove when, still in chains, they were unloaded, now emaciated, half starved and some literally dying.

7

John Mitchel

Probably the most famous convict, if he could be described as such, was John Mitchel. John was a prominent member of the group that had become known as the 'Young Irelanders'. This group had been established by Thomas Davis in 1842. Initially they had been ardent supporters of Daniel O'Connell in his attempts to secure Catholic Emancipation. Their support for him waned however, when they grew frustrated with the lack of progress in his attempts to repeal the Act of Union, which had seen Ireland lose its parliament and come under the jurisdiction of Westminster.

Mitchel had been a contributor to their paper *The Nation* when it was first published in 1842 and had later, in 1848, launched his own paper known as *The United Irishman*. His editorial style and outspoken criticism of British rule was renowned in political circles. He had been highly regarded and had practiced law, but his public utterances were to lead to his eventual arrest. Having suggested that the only way Ireland may achieve independence from Britain was by armed insurrection, he was charged with sedition and received a sentence of fourteen years' transportation to Van Diemen's Land.[67]

He was taken immediately from Dublin to Cork Harbour on the aptly named HMS *Scourge*, to be detained on Spike Island prior to transportation. This was the first leg of a journey that was to take him to the other side of the world. His first impression of Spike Island was that it was a rueful place.

In his book *Jail Journal*, he describes his short stay on Spike and admits throwing himself on his cot in utter despair. Despite his first impression of 'the dark forbidding walls of Spike', he said he was treated kindly there. However this treatment was very much according to his class, both during his short stay on Spike Island and his subsequent voyage to Van Diemen's Land. He was kept separated from the 'common' convicts at all times.

Similarly when he arrived in Hobart he was given the option of an immediate ticket of leave provided he remained in a preset jurisdiction around the town of Bothwell. This is where he stayed and leased a cottage and 200 acres of land, before being joined by his wife. He later escaped and made his way to America.

John Mitchel had been a popular figure. He was accustomed to the hustle and bustle of packed meeting halls, energetic debates and public engagements. But on the evening of Sunday 28 May 1848, this man, considered by some to be a hardened criminal and by others a patriotic hero, flung himself down on a bed and broke into a raging passion of tears. He wept uncontrollably.[68] On this day he was confined and alone, a convict on an island that was to become synonymous with convicts and with transportation. His surroundings comprised of a prison cell sparsely furnished with just a bed, a table, a chair and a nightstand. It overlooked a lonely courtyard inside the walls of the fortress on Spike.

Despite the dismal interior of the fortress, he took solace from the geographical location of the island itself and remarked of his exercise courtyard on the island:

> In this court there is nothing to be seen but the high walls and the blue sky. And beyond these walls I know is the beautiful bay lying in the bosom of its soft green hills. If they keep me here for many years I will forget what the fair outer world is like. Gazing on these grey stones, my eyes will grow stony.[69]

This particular quotation is one of the most misquoted of all comments relating to Spike Island. Many people who worked on Spike Island down through the years have said that Mitchel could not have seen Cobh and

the harbour from his cell, and that his description of
the lovely harbour was fanciful. But as can be seen
from the accurate quotation above, he was saying the
exact opposite, that all he could see was stone. Despite
Mitchel's musings about his conditions on Spike, he
was much better off there than the other inmates. He
had his own cell, was given books to read and was
allowed the privilege of sending a letter. The governor
had even greeted him personally on his arrival. Mitchel
suggests that the fact that the governor knew him was
proof that his sentence was predetermined even before
he stood trial.[70] The governor had also sanctioned the
purchase of a razor and bedclothes for Mitchel, despite
the fact that he was only imprisoned on Spike for four
nights.[71] When Governor Grace advised Mitchel that
he was to be treated differently from everybody else
on his passage to Van Diemen's Land, Mitchel mused
about the definition of felon and posed the question,
if a gentleman and person of education commits a
felony then is he not 'all the more felonious?' Mentally
addressing the British administration he wrote:

If a person of education commits the real crime of
endeavouring to subvert social order, to break down the
sanction of law and to destroy the government under
which he lives (supposing law, order and government to
exist), how does his education entitle him to indulgence
over other felons? But possibly you begin to see, Gaffer

John Bull, that I am no felon at all, and have committed no crime at all, notwithstanding your new 'Act of Parliament', in that case made and provided; and you think it impolitic, or else you are ashamed, to proceed to the uttermost rigour with me. Cowardly John! You ought either not to take up the vigorous policy at all, or carry it through with a high hand. This is child's play. Positively I am either a felon, or you, John are a felon.[72]

This is an interesting discourse on the definition of a felon and is all the more noteworthy for the fact that Mitchel seems oblivious to the situation of the other 'felons' on Spike Island. All convicts were technically there as a result of the famine. The direct quadrupling of the prison population throughout Ireland was a result of the effects of the famine itself. With the prison system unable to cope with this increase, Spike had been opened as a convict depot. Again, many of the detainees at Spike had committed crimes associated with the stealing of food and Mitchel later contended that the 'artificial famine' in Ireland was an act of slaughter:

No sack of Madgeburg, no ravage of the Palatine ever approached the horror and desolation of the slaughters done in Ireland by mere official red tape and stationery and the principles of political economy … the almighty indeed sent the potato blight, but the English created the famine.[73]

Since he was on Spike only seven months after it opened for 'famine convicts' it is difficult to understand why he makes no comment on those incarcerated there in such terrible conditions. He refers to the schoolteacher who taught 'small convicts'[74]; children like Thomas Coyle who, at fourteen years of age, had been sentenced to seven years' transportation for larceny in January 1847. Sent to Spike Island in the interim, he was transported in July 1851. A teenager of sixteen, John Connors was also on Spike while John Mitchel was there. He too was sentenced to seven years' transportation for larceny. Just ten days before John Mitchel arrived on Spike Island, a young lad died, as so many were to do in the ensuing years; Dennis Burns, who had been convicted of 'vagrancy' at the age of eighteen and had been sentenced to ten years' transportation, never left the island.[75]

John Mitchel left within a few days, but many hundreds of others would never leave Spike Island.

8

Mitchel and Van Diemen's Land

Unlike many of the people incarcerated on Spike Island, John Mitchel was removed and transported to Van Diemen's Land. His journey there took eight months, stopping off at Bermuda and South Africa along the way. He was not chained below with the rest of the convicts on his ship.

In Tasmania Mitchel was permitted to live as a gentleman in a location decided by the governor, provided he gave his word he would not try to escape. He agreed and was sent to a small town called Bothwell, towards the central highlands of Tasmania. This area would have been alienating for to any Irishman. The terrain, the vegetation, the wildlife and even the seasons were very different to back home and in stark contrast to his last images of Ireland as he sailed out past Roche's Point in Cork Harbour. He ached for his family and initially rented accommodation over a shop in the tiny village where he was sent. This little shop, known as the 'Bothwell Stores', is still there.

Mitchel was required to present himself weekly for roll-call at a specified location in the town and in this way the local magistrate was kept informed of his presence in the prescribed area. Today Bothwell is still a small town with about 300 inhabitants, many of whom take pride in their knowledge of John Mitchel. On a recent visit there, they were delighted to show this author the actual places where he spent his days. He eventually leased a cottage and 200 acres just outside of the town and brought his wife out to share their life together in Tasmania.

While he was in Bothwell, his Young Irelander colleagues Thomas Francis Meagher and William Smith O'Brien had been sentenced to transportation and they too were sent to Van Diemen's Land. Meagher agreed to the same conditions as Mitchel and was sent to live on the shores of the remote Lake Sorrel, to the north of Bothwell. Even today it can take a two-hour hike through the bush, off a non-paved road, to get to the ruins of his cottage. He lived there with two servants, in the midst of the Tasmanian wilderness.

O'Brien, on the other hand, refused to give his word on the matter of attempting escape and as a result he was assigned to Maria Island off the south-east coast of Tasmania. Although as an island this place is remote, it is nevertheless a place great beauty. It certainly did not have the grey walls or the treeless landscaped shape of Spike Island. Rather, a dominant forest-crowned mountain protects the northern side of the island from the ravages of the Southern Ocean. The island is blessed too with a crescent shaped golden beach that bathes in the sunshine of the southern hemisphere for most of the day. There are cliffs, meadows and ancient trees, all with an abundance of native wildlife. William Smith O'Brien was provided with his own cottage there but despite the island's beauty he passionately missed the company of his own class and was not even permitted to mix with others on the island.

While there he wrote, 'To find a gaol in one of the loveliest spots formed by the hand of God in one of her loneliest solitudes creates revulsion of feeling I cannot describe.' O'Brien did not stay on Maria Island for a very long time. Modern Australian historians refer to a perceived scandal in the making when O'Brien took an interest in the governor's daughter. A feigned escape attempt was enacted where O'Brien walked from the crescent shaped beach towards the water and was 'apprehended by two gaolers'.[76] He was sent to Port Arthur.

Port Arthur was the most dreaded place of all and was usually reserved for those convicts found committing second offences after they had arrived in the colony.

Situated on the southern tip of the Tasman Peninsula, this huge prison complex had no outer walls. There was nowhere for escapees to go, only into the wilderness of the bush. Many convicts down through the years tried to escape by heading off into the bush. Invariably they did not survive and their bodies would be found in the hostile bush that surrounded the area.

The Tasman Peninsula was the perfect place to build Port Arthur. Although it stretches into the Southern Ocean and widens to the south, there is one point at which it narrows to no more than 200 yards, at a place called Eaglehawk Neck. Although confident that no convicts could make it to this northern area of the peninsula in any escape attempt, the authorities nevertheless took no chances. At this narrow point of the peninsula a heavy steel chain was strung across the stretch with a dozen fearsome dogs snarling and ready to devour anyone who approached.

Port Arthur itself was a large complex. It had the main prison, a dockyard, a hospital a lunatic asylum, two churches and a military area where soldiers were housed. Again, William Smith O'Brien was given his own cottage but refused permission to mix with any of the other prisoners. A large wall was built around the cottage itself, depriving him even the sight of other humans. His cottage was on a hill overlooking the bay but like Mitchel on Spike Island, he could only imagine the scene outside. Had he been able to look upon it he would have seen the main prison complex beneath him, with two islands just offshore. One of

1. Seagulls on the shoreline of Spike Island.

2. Pier on the western side of the island.

3. Early monastic site?

4. Smugglers' caves?

5. Northern shoreline, Spike Island

6. The overgrown schoolhouse.

7. Mitchel's Courtyard.

8. The Drill Shed.

9. Married Quarters.

10. Ariel view of Spike Island.

11. Old map showing the location of the convict burial ground.

12. A Celtic cross marks the convict cemetery

13. Detail of the commemorative plaque on the Celtic cross in the convict cemetery.

14. Convict headstones.

15. Fort Mitchel, as seen from the sea.

these, Point Puer, was a prison island for children of fourteen years or less. Tales abound of young boys joining hands and jumping off the small cliffs of the island in desperate suicide pacts. These stories have been strenuously denied by the authorities but they still persist. The other island is simply known as the Isle of the Dead. Any convicts who died at Port Arthur were buried here. It is where hundreds of convicts were buried, again with no headstones and no dignity. Staff at the Port Arthur Visitor Centre were recently struck with the similarities between the arrangements on Spike Island in Cork Harbour and the Isle of the Dead.

O'Brien found it increasingly difficult to endure his isolation. A prison doctor feared that his mental health was suffering. He eventually agreed to the terms of his ticket of leave and was released from Port Arthur to take up residence in a town called New Norfolk in the Derwent Valley, north of Hobart. There he had the freedom of movement and more importantly the ability to mix socially that he had missed so much.

Meanwhile in a remote location called Interlaken, straddled between Lake Sorell and Lake Crescent, where their two jurisdictions bordered each other, Meagher and Mitchel often met secretly. There, in a shepherd's hut they plotted their escape. Unlike thousands of others they were successful and escaped to America, both by different routes. Meagher left his wife Catherine behind in Tasmania. She was heavily pregnant and was to follow him after the child was born. Meagher was never to meet his son, and he never again saw his wife. The infant, Henry Emmet Fitzgerald died aged four months. Catherine returned to Ireland and while awaiting her trip to America, she fell ill and died. The child's grave lies beside the small catholic church of St Johns in Richmond, Tasmania

Meagher and Mitchel also took different sides in the American Civil War. Mitchel wrote articles in defence of the southern states' rights to property and self-determination. Two of his sons fought on the Confederate side, one of whom was wounded at Gettysburg. Thomas Francis Meagher fought with the Army of the Potomac and was involved in the Battle of Bull Run. He later established and led an Irish Brigade, which fought at Fredericksburg and Antietam. He was later appointed secretary of the territory of Montana and served as acting governor.[77] He died in 1867, in somewhat mysterious circumstances on a riverboat on the Missouri River. In Tasmania today a cove of the larger Lake Sorrell is named 'Meaghers Bay' in memory of his time there.

William Smith O'Brien was later pardoned and went back to Europe to live in Paris. Mitchel lived out his life in New York, controversial and opinionated to the end of his days. It had been while there that he published a series of articles accusing the British Government of the deliberate policy of neglect in dealing with the effects of the famine. Interestingly his book *Jail Journal*, which gives an account of his time at Spike Island, does not refer to the famine itself even though he was surrounded during his short stay by young people who were there directly as a result of it. Perhaps, like the judiciary, he saw the convicts merely as criminals and not as victims of what he describes as a man-made catastrophe.

Mitchel, Meagher, and O'Brien found themselves caught up in the system of transportation as a result of their beliefs and political aspirations. Their treatment however was deferential. They were afforded special status in a system that could be often cruel and unforgiving.

9

The End of Transportation

Transportation, as an economic means of ridding Britain of its convicts while at the same time providing a cheap labour force for the building up of her colonies, paused in 1853, when no more felons were sent to Van Diemen's Land. Western Australia, having only been operating as a penal colony since 1850,[78] was then used for a time but the last vessel ever to transport convicts there set sail, carrying sixty-two Fenians, on 2 October 1867.[79] This was the last vessel ever to leave Ireland with convicts and the last one to arrive in a penal colony in Australia.

Shaw argues that it had become much cheaper for Britain to build prisons and keep her convicts at home.[80] The reasoning was not just economic, however, as there had also been colonial opposition to transportation; free settlers did not want their land to be seen as a dumping ground for the dregs of society.

It had also ceased to function as a deterrent as many of those transported had settled down and were doing well. Hughes concentrates significantly on the growing failure of deterrence, although he contends the aims of England in introducing transportation were to sublimate, reform, deter and to colonise. It failed in much of this. He records that Charles Dickens wrote to the Home Secretary in October 1840, telling him that most criminals now thought of 'transportation as a passport to opportunity and even wealth'.[81]

Between 1847 and 1853, ships were still leaving Spike Island for Van Diemen's Land. It would appear that those who did get transported might have been the lucky ones; many of those who remained endured hardship, isolation and death. They met their deaths while in the custody of the State. Whether they died of disease, climate or hard labour will probably be always a matter for debate. Perhaps things went on in Spike that the official records do not reveal. Certainly in the year following the death of over 200 convicts, the Roman Catholic Chaplain alluded to 'defects in the system that were physically and morally destructive'.[82] The ban on correspondence to and from the convicts deprives us of a valuable primary source that may have balanced the blameless official reports. Nevertheless it remains difficult to reconcile the instructions of the Inspector General regarding convicts on Spike Island (and the high mortality rate there) with the conclusions of Stephen Nicholas who claims the convicts of Australia 'received fair treatment, good rations, adequate housing, comprehensive medical care and a reasonable work day and week'.[83] Perhaps the convicts of Cork Harbour would have faired much better in Australia.

Felons or Famine Victims?

Many individuals that were on Spike found themselves categorised as felons but the judicial system of the day took little account of the mitigating circumstances that lead them to stealing potatoes and food. People were starving, some had children to feed, and others were barely children themselves. In the year of 1849 out of a total of 1,435 convictions for which people were on Spike Island, 352 were there for larceny, 280 for cattle stealing, 291 sheep stealing and 15 for pig stealing. These crimes, if perpetrated as a means to acquire food, represent almost 65 per cent of the total. Whatever number were committed in such circumstances were direct victims of the famine. Their actions, driven by hunger and desperation, labelled them forever in officialdom as criminals.

Unlike other establishments such as county and city gaols, whose occupants were drawn from the area in which they were located, Spike Island catered for people from all over the country. In the case of the overcrowding wrought by the special circumstances of the famine it was the spillover, the excess from all other counties, that was sent to Spike. Parts of the country felt the effects of the famine worse than others. A poor relief system set up by a reluctant British Government, which only envisaged ever having to cater to 1 per cent of the population.[84] The reality was very different however. Sometimes up to 50 per cent of the population in certain areas found themselves needing relief. Unlike the British Poor Law, the Poor Law enacted in 1838 for relief in Ireland did not provide a 'right of relief'. If a workhouse was full in England, Scotland or Wales the onus was on officials to provide alternative relief. In Ireland, if a workhouse was full, people were turned away and left to their own devices. In this context it is not surprising that many turned in desperation to stealing and begging.

Those who died as convicts on Spike Island are amongst the forgotten victims of the worst chapter in Ireland's history. The climatic conditions that brought the successive crop failures were beyond their control. Political decisions into which they had no input determined how they would be assisted and by whom. Economic doctrines, with which they were probably unfamiliar, deprived them of the very basic necessities to survive. Their desperate responses in the light of little or no assistance, coupled with the criminalising of begging and homelessness, placed them at the mercy of a system that sent them into judicial oblivion.

Recent Usage

In 1883 the convicts were removed from Spike Island. Some believed that to be the last of the island's association with prisoners, but this was not to be the case.

The British Army, who had been on the island from the late 1700s, used their barracks there as a prison for political suspects during the Irish War of Independence when internment was introduced. Despite Independence being achieved in 1921, Spike remained under the jurisdiction of the British Army under the Treaty, and they finally left on 11 July 1938. The raising of the Irish flag for the first time on Spike Island was performed by the leader of the government, An Taoiseach (prime minister) Éamon de Valera. Although the ceremony itself was brief, the symbolism was evident by the presence of the majority of the government cabinet. Just hours earlier the British Army had officially handed over the star-shaped fortress called Westmoreland to the Irish Army. Only after the last British soldier left the island did de Valera and his ministers embark from Cobh to raise the Irish tricolour.

The new Irish constitution of 1937, inspired by and almost exclusively crafted by de Valera, claimed jurisdiction over the whole of the island of Ireland and its islands. Spike Island presented the opportunity to raise the national flag on soil that had been in the possession of what de Valera saw as an occupying force for almost eight centuries. The fort was renamed Fort Mitchel after its most famous occupant during the famine. The outer forts of Camden and Carlisle were also renamed and another pair of Young Irelanders honoured. The founder of the movement, Thomas Davis, and the colleague, friend, and later rival of Mitchel, Thomas Francis Meagher, both now give their names to the outer forts. Mitchel, Meagher and Davis, once fellow activists in the Young Ireland movement and later separated by early death and the American Civil War, stand together again in the forts of Cork Harbour.

Having taken over in 1938, the Irish Army maintained a presence on the three forts for decades. Forts Meagher and Mitchel are no longer in the possession of the Department of Defence. In 1979 the Army handed Spike Island over to the Irish Naval Service who utilised its isolation as a training academy for recruits and other courses.

In 1984 the Irish Government was under considerable public pressure to do something about the growing anti-social activity of 'joyriding'. This was a crime that was receiving widespread coverage from the media and it involved groups of youths stealing motor vehicles and driving them at dangerous speeds around the urban areas of Ireland's cities. There were numerous deaths and many hundreds of incidences of car theft and destruction. Newspapers and other media outlets highlighted these problems and the government was increasingly criticised for failing to tackle the problem. One of the difficulties faced by the then government was a shortage of juvenile prison space throughout the country. Under increasing pressure from the media they decided to utilise Spike Island as a place of detention. The Naval Service was told to vacate the island and it eventually came under the jurisdiction of the Department of Justice. A prison was opened there with accommodation for over sixty inmates and it operated from 1984 until 2005.

The island today remains under the jurisdiction of that Department and there was indication from Government sources in 2005 that a planned 'super-prison' would eventually be built there. This development was to incorporate among other things, the building of a bridge to the island. It is likely that if this should ever happen, the graves of so many of the victims of Ireland's greatest human catastrophe would be desecrated. It is incumbent on any government and any people to protect the heritage of the country.

Like Cobh and Cork Harbour, the hills, forests and natural formations of Tasmania bare testimony to historical events and to human endeavour and suffering. The crumbling walls of Port Arthur and the lonely beach on Maria Island hold direct connections with our heritage, just like the walls of Spike Island prison and the piers and streets of Cobh.

The Spike Island cell block in which Mitchel was incarcerated is still there today. Over the years there have been disputes about which room he was actually in but the courtyard and blockhouse he describes in his own words are easily identifiable. In Bothwell they also value the historical significance of the presence of John Mitchel in what is still a small rural village.

Direct connections like these are there to be explored. They constitute national heritage. They should fascinate and inspire. The walls that stand on Spike Island in Cork Harbour are the very same ones that were built with the trembling hands of Irish convicts. These form part of the culture of the country and are a part of the people. Places such as America and Australia were moulded by the sweat and suffering of these people. Today, of course, Ireland enjoys better times. Circumstances are much improved but somewhere in the world there are people going through the agony of oppression and the injustice of wrongful separation. Cork has its harbour, its history and its islands as living reminders of Ireland's long journey from the bright days of ecclesiastical excellence, through the dark days of invasion, conquest oppression and struggle.

The wealth of ecclesiastical, military and penal history of Spike Island is interspersed with the experiences of thousands of people with a great diversity of cultural, political and ethnic backgrounds. Only a tiny portion of its rich heritage has been dealt with in this book. So much about this island merits further study and writing; the possibility of an influence on some of the most noted manuscripts in history; the chance that perhaps there is an ethical connection with the Céli Dé; the mystery of the disturbing mortality rates of its convicts. All are testament to the extraordinary historical importance of this island and I have no doubt that continued academic and archaeological investigation of its history will provide fascinating insights into the lives and deaths of those who passed through Spike Island.

Bibliography

Primary Sources

National Archive Ireland:

NAI (accessed online 29/7/07) – See subcategory: 'Spike Island' under Ireland–Australia Transportation Database.

NAI Document TR 6, p.99 accessed online at http://www. nationalarchives.ie on 30 August 2007.

NAI TR7, p.32.

NAI TR7, p.72.

NAI TR9, p.120.

Sources in the National Archives for research into the transportation of Irish convicts to Australia (1791-1853): Introduction

http://www.nationalarchives.ie/topics/transportation/ transp1.html Accessed 7 January 2007

Public Records Office, Kew, London

PRO AO 19/44/12 *Accounts of Governor Richard Grace for 6 months up to September 1848.*

PRO, MPH 191

House of Commons Parliamentary Papers:

HCPP 1805 (91) *Return of Persons confined in Gaols in Ireland under Acts for Detention of Persons suspected of Conspiring against H.M. Government, 1803-04* Vol. VI. 431.

HCPP 1808 (239) *Inspectors General Report on General State of Prisons of Ireland, 1807* Vol. IX. 351.

HCPP 1809 (265) *Coms. of Inquiry into Condition and Government of State Prisons and Gaols in Ireland. Report, Appendix* Vol. VII. 577.

HCPP 1810-11 (180) *Bill to Authorize Punishment by Confinement and Hard Labour of Persons in Ireland liable to Transportation* Vol. I.493.

HCPP 1817 (343) *Coms. on alleged Abuses in Convict Dept. at Cork. Report, Minutes of Evidence* Vol. VIII.99.

HCPP 1819 (534) *Inspectors General, Report on General State of Prisons of Ireland, 1818, Appendix* Vol XII. 453.

HCPP 1821 (172) *Return of Number of Convicts sent from Ireland to New South Wales, 1817-20* Vol. XX 157.

HCPP 1823 (342) *Inspectors General, First Report on General State of Prisons of Ireland* Vol. X.291.

HCPP 1824 (294) *Inspectors General, Second Report* Vol. XXII.269.

HCPP 1825 (493) *Inspectors General, Third Report* Vol. XXII.227.

HCPP 1826 (173) *Inspectors General, Fourth Report* Vol. XXIII.395.

HCPP 1826-27 (471) *Inspectors General, Fifth Report* Vol. XI.335.

HCPP 1828 (68) *Inspectors General, Sixth Report* Vol. XII.349.

HCPP 1829 (10) *Inspectors General, Seventh Report* Vol. XIII.421.

HCPP 1830 (48) *Inspectors General, Eight Report* Vol. XIV.719.

HCPP 1830-31 (172) *Inspectors General, Ninth Report* Vol. IV.269.

HCPP 1831-32 (152) *Inspectors General, Tenth Report* Vol. XXIII.451.

HCPP 1833 (67) *Inspectors General, Eleventh Report* Vol. XVII.307.

HCPP 1833 (101) *Return of Officers employed in Convict Dept. in Ireland; Expense of Maintaining Convicts in Dublin Gaol; Number confined in Kilmainham Gaol* Vol. XXVIII.651.

HCPP 1834 (63) *Inspectors General, Twelfth Report* Vol. XL.69.

HCPP 1835 (114) *Inspectors General, Thirteenth Report* Vol. XXXVI.381.

HCPP 1835 (535) *Account of Expense of Convict Establishment at Cork* Vol. XLV.111.

HCPP 1836 (118) *Inspectors General, Fourteenth Report* Vol. XXXV. 431.

HCPP 1837 (123) *Inspectors General, Fifteenth Report* Vol. XXXI.605.

HCPP 1837-38 (186) *Inspectors General, Sixteenth Report* Vol. XXIX.475.

HCPP 1839 (91) *Inspectors General, Seventeenth Report* Vol. XX.403.

HCPP 1840 (240) *Inspectors General, Eighteenth Report* Vol. XXVII.165.

HCPP 1841 Session 1 (299) *Inspectors General, Nineteenth Report* Vol. XI.759.

HCPP 1842 (377) *Inspectors General, Twentieth Report* Vol. XXII.177.

HCPP 1843 (462) *Inspectors General, Twenty-first Report* Vol. XXVII.83.

HCPP 1844 (535) *Inspectors General, Twenty-second Report* Vol. XXVIII.329.

HCPP 1845 (620) *Inspectors General, Twenty-third Report* Vol. XXV.231.

HCPP 1846 (697) *Inspectors General, Twenty-fourth Report* Vol. XX.257.

HCPP 1847 (805) *Inspectors General, Twenty-fifth Report* Vol. XXIX.151.

HCPP 1847-48 (952) *Inspectors General, Twenty-sixth Report* Vol. XXXIV.253.

HCPP 1849 (1069) *Inspectors General, Twenty-seventh Report* Vol. XXVI.373.

HCPP 1949 (393) *Bill, intituled, Act to remove Doubts concerning Transportation of Offenders under Judgment of Death in Ireland* Vol. VI.547.

HCPP 1850 (1229) *Inspectors General, Twenty-eight Report* Vol. XXIX.305.

HCPP 1851 (1364) *Inspectors General, Twenty-ninth Report* Vol. XXVIII.357.

HCPP 1852 (1429) *Inspector of Government Prisons in Ireland. Annual Report, 1850, Appendices* Vol. XXV.249.

HCPP 1852 (1531) *Inspectors General, Thirtieth Report* Vol. XXV.249.

HCPP 1852-53 (809) *Act to Substitute other Punishment in lieu of Transportation* Vol. VII.429.

HCPP 1852-53 (1634) *Inspector of Government Prisons in Ireland, Annual Report, 1851, Appendices* Vol. LIII.277.

HCPP 1852-3 (412) *Abstract Return of Convicts sentenced to Transportation and Prisoners in County Gaols in Ireland, 1847-51* Vol. LXXXI.238.

HCPP 1854-55 (1958) *Directors of Convict Prisons in Ireland. First Annual Report, 1854* Vol. XXVI.609.

HCPP 1856 (123) *Return of Number of Convicts in Convict Prisons in Ireland, January 1856* Vol. LIII.347.

HCPP 1857 Session 2 (334) *Abstract Return of Convicts sentenced to Transportation and Prisoners in County Gaols in Ireland, 1852-56* Vol. XXXIX.555.

HCPP 1865 (394) *Return of Number of Persons confined in Convict Prisons in Ireland Under Sentence of Penal Servitude* Vol. XLV.729.

HCPP 187X (50) *Papers relating to Case of J. Mitchel (former Proprietor of United Irishmen Newspaper; Escapee from Convict Settlement at Tasmania)* Vol. LXII.165.

All House of Commons Parliamentary Papers were accessed between 15 December 2006 and 27 February 2007 from the online archive at: *http://0-parlipapers.chadwyck.co.uk.innopac.ucc.ie/home.do*

Secondary sources

Broderick, M., *History of Cobh (Queenstown) Ireland* (M. Broderick: Cobh, 1994).

Brunicardi, N., *Haulbowline, Spike and Rocky Islands* (Eigse: Haulbowline, 1968).

Carroll-Burke, P., *Colonial discipline, the making of the Irish convict system* (Four Courts Press: Dublin, 2000).

Carthage, Fr, OCSO, *The Story of Saint Carthage* (Brown & Nolan: Dublin, 1937).

Charbonneau, A.S., *1847 Grosse Île: a record of daily events* (Canadian Government Publishing Centre: Ottawa, 1997).

Charles-Edwards, T.M., *Early Christian Ireland* (Cambridge University Press: Cambridge, 2000).

Costello, Con, *Botany Bay: The Story of the Convicts Transported from Ireland to Australia 1791-1853* (Mercier Press: Cork, 1987).

Dennehy, H.E. & Coleman, J., *History of Great Island, the Cove of Cork and Queenstown* (Tower: Cork, 1990).

Dudley Edwards, R. &Williams, T.D., (eds) *The Great Famine, studies in Irish History 1845-52* (Lilliput: Dublin, 1994).

Griffin, B., *Sources for the study of crime in Ireland* (Four Courts: Dublin, 2005).

Hughes, R., *The Fatal Shore* (Collins Harvill: London, 1987).

Kinealy, C., *This Great Calamity: the Irish Famine 1845-52* (Gill & Macmillan: Dublin, 1994).

King, C., (ed.) *Famine Land and Culture in Ireland* (UCD: Dublin, 2000).

Leland, M., *That Endless Adventure, a History of the Cork Harbour Commissioners* (Port of Cork Co.: Cork, 2001).

Lord, Richard, *The Isle of the Dead Port Arthur* (Lord & Associates: Taroona, 1976).

Maxwell-Stewart, H., & Hood, S., *Pack of Thieves: Fifty-Two Port Arthur Lives* (Port Arthur Historic Site: Port Arthur, 2001).

McConville, S., *Irish Political Prisoners, 1848-1922 Theatres of War* (Routledge: London, 2003).

McConville, S., *A History of English Prison Administration Vol. I 1750-1877* (Routledge: London, 1981).

McVerry, Peter, S.J., *Spike Island: The Answer to What?* (Resource Publications: Dublin, 1984

Mitchel, J., *Jail Journal* (Dublin, 1982).

Mitchel, J., *The Last Conquest of Ireland (perhaps)* (UCD: Dublin, 2005).

Moody, T.W., & Martin, F.X. (eds), *The course of Irish History* (UCD: Dublin, 2000).

Morris, N. & Rothman, D.J., (eds), *The Oxford History of the Prison, the Practice of Punishment in Western Society* (OUP: New York, 1995).

Murray, P., *Maritime paintings of Cork 1700-2000* (Crawford Municipal Art Gallery, the Port of Cork, and Gandon: Cork, 2005).

Nicholas, S., (ed.), *Convict workers: Reinterpreting Australia's Past* (Cambridge University Press: Cambridge, 1989).

O'Callaghan, S., *To Hell or Barbados: The Ethnic Cleansing of Ireland* (Brandon: Kerry, 2000).

O'Dwyer, Peter, O. Carm., *Céli Dé: Spiritual Reform in Ireland 700-900* (Dublin, 1981).

O'Dwyer, Peter, O. Carm., *Towards a History of Irish Spirituality* (Columba Press: Dublin, 1995).

Ó'Gráda, C., *Ireland's Great Famine, Interdisciplinary Perspectives* (UCD: Dublin, 2006).

O'Sullivan, P., (ed.) *The Meaning of the Famine Vol. 6: The Irish World Wide: Heritage and Identity* (Leicester University Press: Leicester, 1997).

Power, P., Revd Trans, *The Life of St Declan of Ardmore and The Life of St Mochuda of Lismore* (Irish Texts Society: London, 1914).

Power, P., Revd Trans, *Life of St Mochuda of Lismore* (edited from Manuscript in Library of Royal Irish Academy: London, 1914).

Priestley, P., *Victorian Prison Lives: English Prison Biography 1830-1914* (Pimlico: London, 1985).

Robins, J., *The Miasma: Epidemic and Fear in Nineteenth-Century Ireland* (Dublin, 1995).

Robson, L.L., *The Convict Settlers of Australia* (Melbourne University Press: Melbourne, 1965).

Rynne, Colin, *The Archaeology of Cork City and Harbour: from the Earliest Times to Industrialisation* (Collins Press: Cork, 1993).

Shaw, A.G.L., *Convicts and the Colonies: a Study of Penal Transportation from Great Britain and Ireland to*

Australia and other parts of the British Empire (Faber & Faber: London, 1966).

Watkins, Tom, Basil, OSB, (ed.), *The Book Of Saints* (7th Edition) (A&C Black: London, 2002).

Woodham Smith, C., *The Great Hunger 1845-9* (Hamish Hamilton: London, 1962).

Articles

Coleman, J., HMC, MRSA 'The Story of Spike Island', *Journal of the Cork Historical and Archaeological Society*, Vol. II, No. 13, 1893.

E. R., Green, 'The Great Famine' *The course of Irish History* (UCD: Dublin, 2000), p.220.

Kennedy, L., 'Bastardy and the Great Famine: Ireland 1845-50', *Famine. Land and Culture in Ireland.*

'Letter to Mr Grace, Governor, Convict Depot Spike Island', *Inspectors general, twenty-sixth report* Vol. XXXIV.253.

Mc Conville, S., 'The Victorian Prison, England 1865-1965', *The Oxford History of the Prison* (OUP: New York, 1995). p.121

Smyth, Marina , 'The date and origin of Liber de creaturarum', *Journal of the Medieval Academy of Ireland* V17-18, 2003-2004, pp.1-38.

Government Publications

Power, Denis (ed.), *Archaeological Inventory of County Cork*, VII (East and South Cork) Stationary Office, Dublin, 1994

National Archive, Online records

http://www.nationalarchives.ie/cgi-bin/naisearch01
http://www.britannica.com/eb/article-9051679

Endnotes

Chapter 2 The Island

1 www.nationalarchives.ie/cgi-bin/naisearch01
2 Power, Revd P., (ed) Lives of Saint Declan and Mochuda (Irish Texts Society: London, 1914).
3 Dr D., Bracken, University College Cork, 2005.
4 Watkins, T.B., OSB, (ed.) *The Book of Saints* (7th Edition) (A&C Black: London, 2002).
5 O'Dwyer, P., *Céli Dé, Spiritual Reform in Ireland 750-900*, (Dublin, 1981), p.xi.
6 O'Dwyer, *Céli Dé*, p.4.
7 O'Dwyer, *Céli Dé*, p.194.
8 O'Dwyer, *Céli Dé*, p.176.
9 Charles-Edwards, T.M., *Early Christian Ireland* (Cambridge University Press: Cambridge, 2000), p.140.
10 Power, Revd P., *Life of St Mochuda of Lismore*, edited from Manuscript in Library of Royal Irish Academy, (London, 1914).

Chapter 3 *The Liber Creaturarum*

[11] Smyth, M., 'The date and origin of Liber de Creaturarum', *Journal of the Medieval Academy of Ireland* V17-18, 2003-2004, p.1-3.

[12] Smyth., p.2 footnote: Paul Grosjean, 'Sur quelques exegetes Irlandais du VII siecle', Sacris Erudiri 7 (1995) pp.67-98. See also Aidan Breen, 'Some Seventh-Century Hiberno-Latin Texts and their Relationships', Peritia 3 (1984) pp.204-14.

[13] Smyth, p.39.

[14] Murray, P., *Maritime Paintings of Cork Harbour 1700-2000* (Crawford Municipal Art Gallery, the Port of Cork, Gandon: Cork, 2005), p.72.

[15] Murray, p.72.

[16] PRO, MPH 191, (Kew, London).

[17] O'Corráin, Prof. D., University College Cork, November 2005.

[18] Coleman refers here to Cardinal Moran's edition of *Archdale's Monasticon Hibernicum*, which outlines the status of Spike Island as a holy island.

[19] Coleman, J.,'The Story of Spike Island' *Journal of the Cork Historical and Archaeological Society*, Vol. II, No. 13, 1893.

[20] Coleman, p.2.

[21] Coleman, p.2.

[22] Power, D. (ed.) *Archaeological Inventory of County Cork*, Volume 2: East and South Cork, (Government Publications Office: Dublin, 1994).

Chapter 4 Changing Usage

[23] Broderick, M., *History of Cobh (Queenstown) Ireland* (M. Broderick: Cobh, 1989), pp.79-80.

[24] O'Callaghan, S., *To Hell or Barbados: The Ethnic Cleansing of Ireland* (Brandon: Kerry, 2000), pp.41-53.

[25] O'Callaghan, p.45.

[26] Coleman, p.5.

Chapter 5 Transportation and the Convicts of Cork Harbour

[27] HCPP 1823 (342) *Inspectors General, First Report on the General State of Prisons in Ireland* Vol. X.291.

[28] Hughes, R., *The Fatal Shore* (Collins Harvill: London, 1987), p.40; Shaw, A.G.L., *Convicts and the Colonies: a Study of Penal Transportation from Great Britain and Ireland to Australia and other parts of the British Empire* (Faber & Faber: London, 1966), p.23.

[29] Nicholas, S., *Convict Workers: Reinterpreting Australia's Past* (Cambridge University Press: Cambridge, 1989), p.24, in which he cites HCPPI 1837, *Report from the Select Committee on Transportation*, Vol. XIX.C518, (Appendix 10), p.258.

[30] O'Callaghan, p.34; Hughes, p.41.

[31] Hughes, p.xi.

[32] http://www.nationalarchives.ie/topics/transportation/transp1.html – Accessed 7 January 2007.

[33] Shaw, p.182.

[34] HCPP 1808 (239), *Inspectors General Report on General State of Prisons in Ireland, 1807* Vol. IX.351.

[35] HCCP 1817 (343) *Commissioner's Report on Alleged Abuses in Convict Depot at Cork.* Report, Minutes of Evidence Vol. VIII.99.

[36] Mc Conville, S., 'The Victorian Prison, England 1865-1965', *The Oxford History of the Prison* (OUP: New York, 1995), p.121.

[37] Art. cit., p.121.

[38] HCPP 1835 (535) *Account of Expense of the Convict Establishment at Cork.* Vol. XLV.111.

[39] HCPP 1828 (68) *Inspectors General, Sixth Report* Vol. XII.394.

[40] HCPP 1810-11 (180) *Bill to Authorize Punishment by Confinement and Hard Labour of Persons in Ireland liable to Transportation* Vol. I.493.

Chapter 6 The Great Famine and Spike Island

[41] Carroll-Burke, P., *Colonial discipline, the making of the Irish convict system* (Four Courts Press: Dublin, 2000), p.95.

[42] Carroll-Burke, p.53., Mc Conville, S. 'The Victorian prison, England 1865-1965', p.123; Priestley, P., *Victorian Prison Lives: English Prison Biography 1830-1914* (Pimlico: London, 1985), p.6.; McConville, S., *A History of English Prison Administration* Vol.I 1750-1877 (Routledge: London, 1981), pp.135-169.

[43] HCPP 1845 (620) *Inspectors General, Twenty-third Report* Vol. XXV.231.

[44] Ó'Gráda,C., *Ireland's Great Famine,Interdisciplinary Perspectives* (UCD: Dublin, 2006), p.16.

[45] Ó'Gráda, p.7.

[46] Dudley Edwards, R. & T. D. Williams (eds), *The Great Famine, studies in Irish History 1845-52* (Lilliput: Dublin, 1994), p.89: Green, E.R., 'The Great Famine', *The Course of Irish History* (UCD: Dublin, 2000), p.220.

[47] Charbonneau, A.S., *1847 Grosse Île: a record of daily events* (Canadian Government Publishing Centre: Ottawa, 1997), pp.3-13.

[48] Kennedy, L. 'Bastardy and the Great Famine: Ireland 1845-50', *Famine Land and Culture in Ireland* (UCD: Dublin, 2000), p.7.

[49] HCPP 1847-48 (952) *Inspectors General, Twenty- sixth Report* Vol. XXXIV.253.

50 Mass convict transportation ceased to Van Diemen's Land in 1847, although a new penal colony established in Western Australia in 1850 operated until transportation finally finished in 1867.

51 C., Ó Gráda, p.59.

52 HCPP 1847 (282), *Act to make Provision for the Punishment of Vagrants and Persons Offending against the Laws in Force for the Relief of the Destitute in Ireland* Vol. III.403.

53 HCPP 1847 (282) Vol. III.403.

54 NAI (accessed online 29/7/07) see subcategory 'Spike Island' under Ireland-Australia transportation database.

55 NAI Document TR 6, p.99 accessed online at http://www.nationalarchives.ie on 30 August 2007.

56 NAI TR7, p.32.

57 NAI TR7, p.72.

58 NAI TR9, p.120.

59 Inspectors Twenty-sixth report points out that under no circumstances could two men be placed in a cell together.

60 HCPP 1847-48 (952) *Inspectors general, Twenty-sixth Report* Vol. XXXIV.253.

61 Robins, J., *The Miasma: Epidemic and Fear in Nineteenth-Century Ireland* (Dublin, 1995), p.127.

62 HCPP 1854-55 (1958) *Director of Convict Prisons in Ireland. First Annual Report, 1854* Vol. XXVI.609.

63 Letter to Mr Grace, Governor, Convict Depot Spike Island, HCCP 1847-48 (952) *Inspectors General, twenty-sixth report* Vol. XXXIV.253.

64 Lord, R., *The Isle of the Dead: Port Arthur* (Lord& Associates: Taroona, 1976), p.3.

65 Coleman, p.6.

66 Coleman, p.6.

Chapter 7 John Mitchel

67 Now Tasmania.

68 Mitchel, J., *Jail Journal* (Dublin, 1982) p.9. First published in New York, 1854.

69 Mitchel, *Jail Journal* p.10.

70 Mitchel, *Jail Journal* p.9.

71 PRO AO 19/44/12 *Accounts of Governor Richard Grace for 6 months up to September 1848.*

72 Mitchel, *Jail Journal* pp.12-13.

73 Mitchel, *The Last Conquest of Ireland (perhaps)*, (UCD: Dublin, 2005), pp.218-219. First published in Glasgow, 1861.

74 Mitchel, *Jail Journal* p.11.

75 NAI http://www.nationalarchives.ie/topics/transportation/transp1.html – accessed 29 July 2007.

Chapter 8 Mitchel and Van Diemen's Land

76 Related to author at Maria Island and Port Arthur in May 2002.

77 *Encyclopedia Britannica*. Retrieved 9 September 2007, from Encyclopedia Britannica Online: http://www.britannica.com/eb/article-9051679

Chapter 9 The End of Transportation

78 Costello, C., *Botany Bay: The Story of the Convicts Transported from Ireland to Australia 1791-1853* (Mercier: Cork, 1987), p.155.

79 Shaw, p.358.

80 Shaw, p.349. Shaw maintains it cost the state £100 per convict per year if transported, while they could be accommodated for just £15 per annum in the prisons at home.

81 Hughes, p.584.

[82] HCPP 1854-55 (1958) *Director of Convict Prisons in Ireland. First Annual Report* Vol. XXVI.609.

[83] Nicholas, p.196.

[84] Kinealy, C., *This Great Calamity: The Irish Famine 1845-52* (Gill & Macmillan: Dublin, 1994), p.21.